COOKING
AHEAD

STEP-BY-STEP COOKING SERIES

COOKING AHEAD

BARRON'S
Woodbury, New York • Toronto

First U.S. and Canadian edition published 1986
by Barron's Educational Series, Inc.

Text copyright © 1985 by The National Magazine Company Limited
Illustrations copyright © 1985 by The National Magazine Company Limited

All inquiries should be addressed to:
Barron's Educational Series, Inc.
113 Crossways Park Drive
Woodbury, New York 11797

International Standard Book No. 0-8120-5685-3

Library of Congress Catalog Card No. 85-26779

Library of Congress Cataloging-in-Publication Data
Main entry under title:

Cook ahead.

(Step-by-step cooking series)
Includes index.
1. Cookery.
TX715.C78248   1986   641.5′55   85-26779
ISBN 0-8120-5685-3

Illustrations: John Woodcock and Kate Simunek
Photography: Melvin Grey
Food Styling: Susanna Tee, Maxine Clark, Janet Smith

Printed in Italy

5 6 7 8   9 8 7 6 5 4 3 2 1

CONTENTS

COOKING NOTES

KITCHEN TIPS

All spoon measures are level unless otherwise stated. All fruits and vegetables are medium size, unless indicated.

- Large eggs should be used, except when otherwise stated.
- Granulated sugar is used, unless otherwise indicated.
- Flour is all-purpose, pre-sifted, unless otherwise mentioned.

Some recipes call for self-rising flour. This flour is available in all supermarkets, but if desired, for each cup of self-rising flour you can substitute 1 cup of all-purpose flour and 1 teaspoon baking soda.

> All recipes in this book serve SIX PEOPLE unless otherwise indicated.

FOR CANADIAN COOKS

The ingredients in this book are given for U.S. customary measuring units. Cooks in Canada must consider the differing types of flour available to them and adjust cake recipes accordingly. Use the following measurements as a general guide:

> 1 U.S. cup = 236 mL or 8 fluid ounces
> 1 Canadian cup = 250 mL
> 1 tablespoon butter = 15 g or $\frac{1}{2}$ ounce
> 1 cup butter = 225 g or 8 ounces
> 1 cup all-purpose flour = 150 g or 5 ounces
> 1 cup granulated sugar = 190 g or $6\frac{1}{2}$ ounces
> 1 cup confectioners sugar = 80 g or $2\frac{2}{3}$ ounces

KEY TO SYMBOLS

`1.00*` Indicates minimum preparation and cooking times in hours and minutes. They do not include prepared items in the list of ingredients; calculated times apply only to the method. An asterisk * indicates extra time should be allowed, so check the note below symbols.

Chef's hats indicate degree of difficulty of a recipe: no hat means it is straightforward; one hat slightly more complicated; two hats indicates that it is for more advanced cooks.

$ Indicates a recipe which is good value for money; $ $ indicates an expensive recipe. No $ sign indicates an inexpensive recipe.

✳ Indicates that a recipe will freeze. If there is no symbol, the recipe is unsuitable for freezing. An asterisk * indicates special freezer instructions, so check the note immediately below the symbols.

`309 cals` Indicates calories per serving, including any serving suggestions (for example, cream, to serve) given in the list of ingredients.

COOK AHEAD

Cooking ahead is sensible and practical—but this doesn't mean that cook-ahead recipes need be uninspiring. In this book there are Soups and Appetizers, Main Meals, Vegetables and Salads, Desserts and Baking ideas. It's an exciting collection of recipes, all of which can be prepared and cooked hours, even days, ahead of time. This is the perfect book to help you make everyday meals with a minimum of effort, and to make entertaining as relaxed as possible.

In the recipe section of the book, every dish is photographed in color, with step-by-step illustrations to guide you smoothly through the preparation. Detailed instructions are provided on preparing and cooking in advance, plus separate sections on the final touches to make before serving—at-a-glance information that all busy cooks will find an absolute boon.

In the tinted pages at the end of the book, there's information to help you with cook-ahead meals, plus basic recipes which form a useful reference section. There's lots of detail on ingredients and equipment, menu planning, preserving and freezing—plus a special section for Christmas, one of the most important occasions in the year when cooking ahead really comes into its own.

Soups and Appetizers

When you're entertaining, it's best to get the first course made in advance, then you can concentrate all your efforts on last-minute things like vegetables and salads, which are best served absolutely fresh. In this chapter you will find soups and appetizers that can be made at least the day before required—so there should be no panic on the night!

TERRINE OF CHICKEN WITH WINE

2.30* $ | 289–362 cals

* plus 6 hours chilling

Serves 8–10

1 lb boneless chicken breasts

6 oz bacon

2 Tbsp butter

3 Tbsp flour

$\frac{2}{3}$ cup dry white wine

2 eggs

$1\frac{1}{2}$ tsp salt

freshly ground pepper

1 Tbsp fresh rosemary, crushed;
    or 1 tsp dried

1 Tbsp lemon juice

1 large garlic clove, crushed

1 lb ground pork

rosemary sprigs, to garnish

1 *To prepare* (2 hours): Remove the skin from the chicken and discard. Slice the breasts across into thin escalopes. Finely chop the bacon.

2 Melt the butter in a saucepan, add the flour and cook over low heat, stirring with a wooden spoon, for 2 minutes. Gradually blend in the wine, stirring after each addition to prevent lumps forming. Bring to the boil slowly, then simmer for 2–3 minutes, stirring.

3 Cool the sauce, then stir in the remaining ingredients except the chicken. Work well together.

4 In a 6-cup loaf tin, layer the chicken and the pork mixture, beginning with chicken and ending with pork.

5 Cover the dish with foil and place in a roasting tin. Pour in enough boiling water to come halfway up the sides of the dish.

6 Bake in the oven at 325°F for $1\frac{1}{2}$ hours. Remove from the roasting tin and cool slightly, then place heavy weights on top of the foil covering. Leave until cold, then chill in the refrigerator for at least 6 hours.

7 *To serve* (30 minutes): Remove the weights and foil covering from the terrine and drain off surplus juices. Leave at room-temperature for 30 minutes before serving. Garnish with rosemary sprigs.

Menu Suggestion
Serve this attractive layered pâté for a special occasion with hot rolls or French bread, and a bottle of Chablis.

FRENCH GARLIC PÂTÉ

2.50* ✳* 646 cals

* plus cooling and chilling after cooking; freeze after cooling in step 7

Serves 8

16 meaty strips bacon

1 lb pork liver

1 lb ground pork

8 oz pork back fat (see box)

French bread (baguette), crusts removed

4 garlic cloves

2 Tbsp anchovy paste

3 Tbsp brandy

2 tsp dried thyme

¼ tsp grated nutmeg

1 egg, beaten

salt and freshly ground pepper

sprigs of thyme, to garnish

1 To prepare (2 hours 45 minutes): Stretch the bacon strips with the flat of a knife blade.

2 Use the bacon strips to line the base and sides of a 6-cup terrine or other ovenproof dish. Reserve enough bacon to cover the top.

3 Grind the liver, meat and fat with the bread and garlic (or work in a food processor if you prefer a pâté with a finer texture).

4 Turn the mixture into a bowl and add the remaining ingredients, with ½ tsp salt and pepper to taste. Beat well to mix.

5 Spoon the mixture into the lined terrine, pressing it down well and leveling the surface. Cover the top of the pâté with the reserved bacon strips, then cover the terrine loosely with foil.

6 Place the terrine in a roasting tin, then pour in enough boiling water to come halfway up the sides of the terrine. Bake in the oven at 325°F for 2 hours. Remove from the roasting tin and pour off any excess fat from the sides of the terrine.

7 Place heavy weights on top of the foil covering (to compress the pâté and make it easier to slice). Leave until cold, then chill for at least 24 hours (or up to 3 days).

8 To serve (5 minutes): Remove the weights and foil covering from the terrine. Loosen the pâté from the terrine by running a knife around the sides, then turn the pâté out on to a serving plate. Cut a few slices just before serving and garnish with thyme.

Menu Suggestion
This strongly flavored pâté is best eaten with fresh crusty French bread and a full-bodied French red wine such as a Côte du Rhône.

FRENCH GARLIC PÂTÉ

Fat is essential in pâtés to achieve moistness and richness. Pork back fat is used in French pâtés because it is smoother and firmer than other animal fats, and tastes good when served cold. Buy pork back fat from your butcher, telling him what you are going to use it for. He might sell it to you in the sheet, with the rind still attached, in which case chill it in the refrigerator to firm the fat before dealing with it. Place the sheet, rind side down, on a board or work surface. With a long sharp knife, work horizontally between the rind and the fat, lifting the fat up and away from the rind as you go along.

Discard the rind and chop the fat before grinding it with the liver and meat.

NUTTY CAMEMBERT PÂTÉ

| 0.20* | ✳* | 315–475 cals |

* plus overnight chilling; freeze at the end of step 3

Serves 4–6

6 oz soft ripe Camembert cheese
8 oz cream cheese
½ tsp paprika
salt and freshly ground pepper
¾ cup finely chopped blanched almonds
extra paprika, to serve

4 Loosen the pâté from the dish by running a knife between the two. Turn the pâté out upside down on to a serving plate and peel off the lining paper. Chill overnight.

1 *To prepare* (15 minutes): Cut the rind off the Camembert, then work the cheese through a sieve into a bowl, or mix in a food processor until smooth.

2 Add the cream cheese, paprika and seasoning to taste. Beat vigorously with a wooden spoon to combine the ingredients well.

3 Spoon the pâté into a greased and parchment-paper–lined 1½-cup dish or mold. Press down well and smooth the surface with the back of the spoon. Cover the dish and freeze for 1 hour.

5 *To serve* (5 minutes): Sprinkle the nuts over the pâté, then press evenly over the top and around the sides with the knife. Sprinkle with paprika. Serve chilled.

Menu Suggestion
Cheese makes an unusual starter. Serve this creamy pâté with wholewheat toast, crispbreads or crackers.

SMOKED TROUT MOUSSE IN LEMON SHELLS

| 1.00* | ✶* | 197 cals |

* plus cooling, and chilling for at least 4 hours or overnight; freeze at the end of step 7

Serves 6

one 8 oz smoked trout

6 large, even-sized lemons

1¼ cups milk

few slices each of onion and carrot

1 bay leaf

4–6 peppercorns

1½ tsp unflavored gelatine

2 Tbsp butter or margarine

2 Tbsp flour

1 Tbsp prepared horseradish

6 Tbsp heavy cream, whipped

1 egg white

salt and freshly ground pepper

chopped fresh parsley and sprigs of fresh herbs, to serve

1 To prepare (55 minutes): Skin the trout and flake the flesh, discarding any bones. Cover and set aside.

2 Cut the lemons in half lengthwise and scoop out all the flesh and membranes with a sharp-edged teaspoon; reserve the shells. Measure 4 Tbsp lemon juice, pour into a small heatproof bowl and reserve.

3 Bring the milk to the boil in a saucepan with the onion, carrot, bay leaf and peppercorns. Remove from the heat, cover and leave to infuse while preparing the mousse mixture.

4 Sprinkle the gelatine over the reserved measured lemon juice. Leave for 5 minutes until spongy, then stand the bowl in a pan of gently simmering water and heat until dissolved.

5 Melt the butter or margarine in a separate saucepan. Sprinkle in the flour and cook, stirring, for 1–2 minutes. Strain in the infused milk a little at a time, whisking vigorously until smooth. Simmer gently for 2 minutes, then turn into a bowl and stir in the liquid gelatine. Leave to cool.

6 Fold the flaked fish into the cold sauce with the horseradish and whipped cream. Whisk the egg white until stiff, then fold in until evenly incorporated. Add seasoning, taking care not to add too much salt because the trout may be quite salty.

7 Spoon the mousse into the hollowed-out lemon shells, then chill in the refrigerator for at least 4 hours, or overnight if more convenient.

8 To serve (5 minutes): Arrange 2 lemon shells on each of 6 serving plates garnished with chopped parsley and a sprig of herbs. Serve chilled.

Menu Suggestion

These make elegant appetizers for a special dinner party. Follow with a main course of Turkey Casserole with Red Wine (page 47) and Coffee Bavarian Cream (page 77) for dessert.

SMOKED TROUT MOUSSE IN LEMON SHELLS

If you are short of time and prefer not to serve this deliciously rich and creamy mousse in the lemon shells, it can be served simply in a large soufflé dish or individual ramekins. White china looks very pretty with the pale color of the mousse, and you can garnish the tops with delicate "butterflies" of sliced lemon. Cut a lemon into thin slices, then cut out opposite quarters, leaving the flesh intact in the middle. Press a small sprig of parsley or other herb into the center.

STUFFED MUSHROOMS

| 1.05* | ⬠ | ✳* | 642 cals |

* plus 1 hour or overnight chilling;
freeze mushrooms and the dip
separately in step 6

Serves 4

| 2 Tbsp olive oil |
| 1 small onion, chopped |
| 2 garlic cloves, crushed |
| 14 oz can tomatoes |
| 1 tsp dried oregano |
| 1 tsp dried basil |
| 2 Tbsp chopped fresh parsley |
| $\frac{1}{4}$ tsp sugar |
| salt and freshly ground pepper |
| 32 even-sized button mushrooms, wiped |
| $\frac{3}{4}$ cup unsalted butter, softened |
| 2 oz can anchovies in olive oil, drained and chopped |
| finely grated rind of 1 lemon |
| 2 eggs, beaten |
| 1 cup dried breadcrumbs |
| vegetable oil for deep frying |

1 *To prepare* (40 minutes): Make the tomato dip. Heat the oil in a saucepan, add the onion and half the garlic and fry gently for 5 minutes until soft but not colored.

2 Add the tomatoes, dried herbs, half the parsley, the sugar and seasoning to taste. Bring to the boil, stirring constantly with a wooden spoon to break up the tomatoes. Lower the heat and simmer, covered, for 30 minutes, stirring occasionally.

3 Meanwhile pull the stems carefully from the mushrooms with your fingers. Chop the stems finely, then place in a bowl with the butter, anchovies, lemon rind, remaining garlic and parsley. Beat the ingredients together until well combined, then add pepper to taste (do not add salt because of the saltiness of the anchovies).

4 Spoon the butter mixture into the cavity of each of the mushrooms.

5 Sandwich the mushrooms together in pairs and pierce through the center of each pair with a wooden toothpick. Dip the mushrooms in the beaten eggs, then in the breadcrumbs until evenly coated.

6 Chill in the refrigerator for 1 hour, or overnight if more convenient. Remove the tomato dip from the heat, leave to cool, then chill in the refrigerator at the same time as the mushrooms.

7 *To serve* (25 minutes): Work the tomato dip in a blender or food processor, then sieve to remove the tomato seeds. Taste and adjust seasoning, then pour into a serving bowl. Return to the refrigerator while frying the mushrooms.

8 Heat the oil in a deep frier to 375°F and deep fry the mushrooms in batches for about 5 minutes until golden brown and crisp on all sides. Drain quickly on absorbent paper, then remove the toothpicks. Serve immediately, with the chilled tomato dip handed separately.

Menu Suggestion
This dinner party appetizer is so substantial that it needs no accompaniment other than chilled dry white wine.

HADDOCK AND SHRIMP GRATINÉE

| 0.50 | $ | 175 cals |

Serves 8

1 lb haddock fillet, skinned
2 Tbsp butter
1 large onion, finely chopped
2 Tbsp flour
1¼ cups milk
2 Tbsp dry white wine
6 oz frozen shrimp, thawed
3 oz Gruyère or mature Cheddar
    cheese, grated
salt and freshly ground pepper
chopped fresh parsley, to garnish

1 To prepare (20 minutes): Cut the haddock fillet into 12 small strips. Fold strips in half and place two each in 6 individual ramekin or gratin dishes.

2 Melt the butter in a saucepan, add the onion and fry gently until soft. Add the flour and cook over low heat, stirring with a wooden spoon, for 2 minutes. Remove the pan from the heat and gradually blend in the milk and wine, stirring after each addition to prevent lumps forming. Bring to the boil slowly, then simmer for 2–3 minutes, stirring.

3 Remove the sauce from the heat, add the shrimp and ½ cup of the cheese with seasoning to taste.

4 Spoon a little sauce into each ramekin, to cover the fish. Sprinkle the remaining cheese on top. Cool and chill in the refrigerator until required.

5 To serve (30 minutes): Bake in the oven at 375°F for 30 minutes. Serve immediately garnished with chopped parsley.

Menu Suggestion
Serve this hot, bubbling appetizer with French bread and chilled dry white wine.

HADDOCK AND SHRIMP GRATINÉE

Haddock has a mild flavor and fairly firm texture, so is a good choice for this dinner party dish. A more expensive fish which can also be used is monkfish—now becoming available at most good fishmongers. Monkfish tastes similar to lobster and has very firm, meaty flesh, ideal for gratinée dishes such as this one, and for kabobs, casseroles and fish pies. For this recipe, buy monkfish fillets, then dice them rather than cutting them into strips.

STUFFED COD CRÊPES

| 1.40 | 🛋 | $ | ✳ | 541 cals |

Serves 6

1 cup flour, plus 3 Tbsp

½ cup salted peanuts, very finely chopped

2 eggs

1 Tbsp vegetable oil

2 cups milk and water mixed

1½ lb cod fillets

2¼ cups milk

4 Tbsp butter

1 cup chopped celery

1 tsp curry powder

salt and freshly ground pepper

5 Tbsp light cream

½ cup grated Cheddar cheese

chopped fresh parsley, to garnish

1 *To prepare* (1 hour): Make the batter for the crêpes. Whisk 1 cup flour, the chopped peanuts, eggs, oil and half the milk and water mixture until quite smooth. Whisk in the remaining liquid.

2 Make twelve 8-inch crêpes in the usual way (see page 156). Keep covered.

3 Wash and dry the fish and place in a large sauté or deep frying pan with the milk. Cover and poach gently for about 12 minutes until the fish is quite tender and begins to flake. Strain off and reserve the liquid. Flake the fish, discarding any bones.

4 Melt the butter in a heavy-based saucepan, add the celery and curry powder and fry gently for 1 minute, stirring. Remove from the heat and stir in the remaining flour, reserved liquid from cooking the fish and seasoning to taste. Bring to the boil, stirring; simmer for 1 minute. Remove from the heat and fold in the cream and flaked fish.

5 Divide the filling between the crêpes, roll up and place side by side in a single layer in a greased shallow ovenproof dish. Sprinkle the grated cheese over the top and cover loosely with foil. Chill in the refrigerator until required.

6 *To serve* (40 minutes): Bake in the oven at 350°F for about 40 minutes. Serve piping hot, sprinkled with chopped parsley.

Menu Suggestion
This is a substantial appetizer, which should be served on its own. Follow with a light main course such as Marinated Lamb Chops (page 30) and a fresh fruity salad for dessert.

CHILLED RATATOUILLE

0.45* | $ | ✳ | 142 cals

* plus 30 minutes cooling and 4 hours chilling

Serves 6

1 large eggplant, about 12 oz in weight
salt and freshly ground pepper
1 lb small zucchini
8 oz trimmed leeks
1 lb tomatoes
1 green pepper
4 Tbsp vegetable oil
4 oz button mushrooms, wiped
$\frac{2}{3}$ cup chicken stock
2 Tbsp tomato paste
1 Tbsp chopped fresh rosemary, or $\frac{1}{2}$ tsp dried

1 *To prepare* (40 minutes): Wipe the eggplant, discard the ends and cut the flesh into large fork-sized pieces.

2 Put the eggplant pieces in a colander or sieve, sprinkle liberally with salt and set aside to drain for 30 minutes.

3 Rinse under cold running water and pat dry with absorbent paper.

4 Wipe the zucchini and slice diagonally into $\frac{1}{4}$ inch thick pieces, discarding the ends.

5 Cut the leeks across into similar sized pieces, discarding the root ends and any tough dark leaves. Wash, pushing the slices apart, and drain well.

6 Skin and quarter the tomatoes; push out the seeds into a nylon sieve placed over a bowl. Reserve the tomato juice. Halve each tomato quarter lengthwise. Slice the pepper into narrow strips, discarding the seeds.

7 Heat the oil in a large sauté or frying pan. Add the eggplant and zucchini and fry over high heat for 2–3 minutes, turning frequently. Stir in the remaining vegetables with the chicken stock, tomato paste, reserved tomato juice, rosemary and seasoning to taste.

8 Bring the contents of the pan to the boil, cover and simmer for 8–10 minutes. The vegetables should be just tender with a hint of crispness, not mushy. Adjust the seasoning and pour out into a bowl to cool for 30 minutes. Chill well in the refrigerator for at least 4 hours.

9 *To serve* (5 minutes): Taste and adjust seasoning, then turn into a large serving bowl or individual dishes. Serve chilled.

Menu Suggestion

Serve for a dinner party appetizer with hot garlic bread. Marinated Lamb Chops (page 30) would make a good main course to follow, with Raspberry Almond Tart (page 67) for dessert.

CHILLED RATATOUILLE

Ratatouille is known more as a hot vegetable dish than as a chilled starter, yet in France it is often served cold, as part of a mixed hors d'oeuvre. French cooks use leftover ratatouille from the day before, which has chilled overnight in the refrigerator to add color and flavor to *hors d'oeuvre variés*. In fact, you will find that ratatouille always tastes better if it has been kept overnight before serving—even if you are serving it as a hot vegetable accompaniment (it goes particularly well with roast lamb or grilled lamb chops with rosemary).

Ratatouille originated in Provence, in the sunny south of France, where all the colorful summer vegetables grow in such profusion. There are literally hundreds of different versions, some of which are pungent with garlic and onions—two of the most prominent Provençal vegetables.

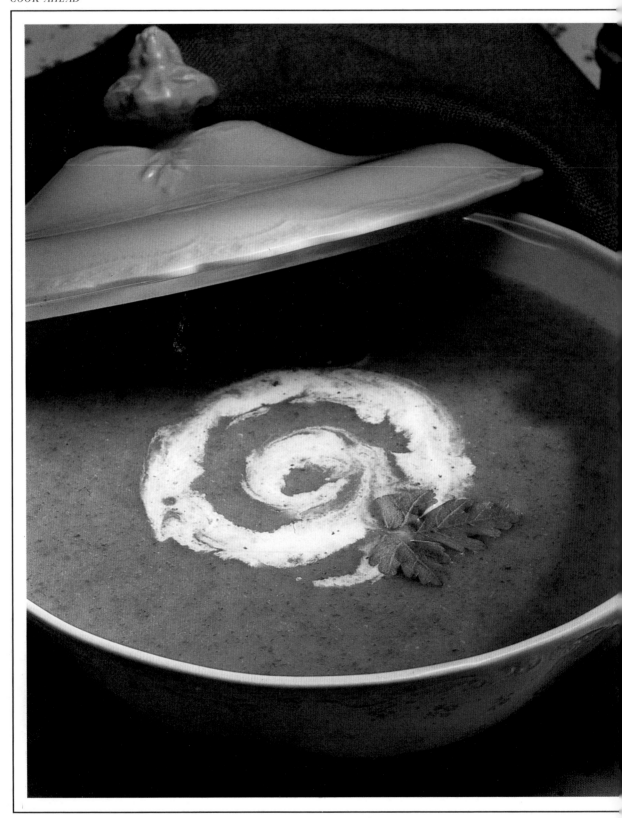

CREAM OF PARSLEY SOUP

| 0.55 | $ | ✳ | 125 cals |

Serves 8

8 oz parsley

2 large onions

2 stalks celery, washed and trimmed

4 Tbsp butter or margarine

3 Tbsp flour

8–9 cups chicken stock, preferably jellied homemade (see page 154)

salt and freshly ground pepper

$\frac{2}{3}$ cup light cream

parsley sprigs, to garnish

1 To prepare (45 minutes): Wash the parsley, drain and chop roughly. Slice the onions and celery.

2 Melt the fat in a large saucepan and add the parsley, onions and celery. Cover the pan and cook gently for about 10 minutes until the vegetables are quite soft. Shake the pan from time to time.

3 Stir in the flour until smooth, then mix in the stock. Add seasoning to taste and bring to the boil.

4 Cover the pan and simmer for 25–30 minutes. Cool a little, then purée in a blender or food processor. Leave to cool completely, then chill in the refrigerator until required.

5 To serve (10 minutes): Reheat until bubbling, taste and adjust seasoning and swirl in the cream. Serve immediately, garnished with the parsley.

Menu Suggestion
Serve this creamy soup in summer when there is plenty of fresh parsley in the garden. Hot French bread or garlic bread would make the perfect accompaniment.

CREAM OF PARSLEY SOUP

This soup can be made in next to no time if you have a food processor. Simply put the parsley, onions and celery in together and chop finely, then add the butter or margarine, flour and stock and work to a smooth purée. Transfer to a saucepan and bring to the boil, stirring constantly until thickened. Lower the heat and simmer as in the recipe. If you like, you can work the soup in the machine again before serving for a really velvety smooth texture.

CURRIED PARSNIP AND ORANGE SOUP

| 0.55* | $ | ✳* | 276 cals |

* plus cooling and overnight standing;
freeze after blending in step 3

Serves 4

4 Tbsp butter or margarine

2 medium parsnips, peeled and
    diced

1 medium onion, chopped

1 garlic clove, crushed

1 tsp curry powder

1 tsp ground cumin

1 Tbsp flour

5 cups chicken stock (see page 154)

finely grated rind and juice of 2
    large oranges

salt and freshly ground pepper

$\frac{2}{3}$ cup light cream, to serve

1 To prepare (45 minutes): Melt the butter or margarine in a large heavy-based saucepan. Add the parsnips and onion, cover the pan and fry gently for about 10 minutes until softened, shaking the pan frequently.

2 Add the garlic and spices and fry, uncovered, for 2 minutes, stirring constantly to prevent burning. Stir in the flour and cook for a further 2 minutes, then pour in the stock and the orange juice. Bring to the boil, stirring, then add seasoning to taste. Lower the heat, cover and simmer for about 20 minutes until the parsnips are tender.

3 Work the soup in a blender or food processor until smooth, then turn into a bowl, cover and leave overnight in a cool place or the refrigerator until cold, to allow the flavors to develop.

4 To serve (10 minutes): Reheat the soup until bubbling, then lower the heat, stir in half the cream and heat through without boiling. Taste and adjust the seasoning.

5 Pour the hot soup into a warmed tureen or individual bowls, swirl with the remaining cream and sprinkle with the grated orange rind. Serve immediately.

Menu Suggestion
This soup makes an unusual dinner party appetizer served with crisp crackers. Follow with Pork with Cider and Coriander (page 36) for the main course and Iced Orange Sabayon (page 79) for the dessert.

ICED ZUCCHINI SOUP

0.40* ✱* 260 cals

* plus cooling and overnight chilling; freeze at the end of step 3

Serves 4

4 Tbsp butter or margarine

1 lb zucchini, trimmed and chopped

1 medium potato, peeled and diced

3¼ cups vegetable stock or water

1 tsp chopped fresh basil or ½ tsp dried basil

salt and freshly ground pepper

4 oz ripe Blue Brie

sliced zucchini, to serve (optional)

1 To prepare (35 minutes): Melt the butter or margarine in a large heavy-based saucepan. Add the zucchini and potato, cover the pan and fry gently for about 10 minutes until softened, shaking frequently.

2 Add the stock or water with the basil and seasoning to taste. Bring to the boil, stirring, then lower the heat and simmer for 20 minutes until the vegetables are tender.

3 Remove the rind from the Brie and chop the cheese into small dice. Put into a blender or food processor, then pour in the soup. Blend until smooth, then turn into a bowl, cover and leave until cold. Chill in the refrigerator overnight.

4 To serve (5 minutes): Whisk the soup vigorously to ensure an even consistency, then taste and adjust seasoning. Pour into a chilled soup tureen or individual bowls and float the zucchini slices on the top if desired.

Menu Suggestion
The perfect appetizer for a summer dinner party or barbecue. Follow with Summer Fish Hot Pot (page 48) and finish with Blackberry Ice Cream (page 78).

Main Meals

The main course of any meal is obviously important. If the main course isn't a success, then most guests will remember the whole meal as a disaster. The cook-ahead dishes in this chapter are designed to help you get it right every time. With the main course organized in advance, there will be no last-minute panic or rush, and meat dishes such as casseroles will be greatly improved in flavor.

LAMB AND ORANGE CASSEROLE WITH PASTRY DUMPLINGS

3.25* ✳* 790 cals

* plus cooling overnight; freeze at the end of step 4

Serves 4

3 Tbsp vegetable oil

2 lb lean boned leg of lamb, trimmed of fat and cubed

1 medium onion, chopped

2 turnips, peeled and roughly chopped

3 carrots, roughly chopped

$\frac{1}{2}$ cup flour

1 Tbsp tomato paste

$1\frac{1}{4}$ cups unsweetened orange juice

$\frac{2}{3}$ cup chicken stock

2 bay leaves

salt and freshly ground pepper

4 Tbsp butter

$\frac{2}{3}$ cup water

2 eggs, beaten

finely grated rind of 2 oranges

2 Tbsp chopped fresh parsley and orange shreds, to garnish

1 *To prepare* (2 hours): Heat the oil in a large flameproof casserole, add the lamb in batches and fry over brisk heat until browned on all sides. Remove with a slotted spoon and set aside.

2 Add the onion to the casserole, lower the heat and fry gently for 5 minutes until soft but not colored. Add the turnips and carrots and fry for a further 5 minutes, stirring constantly.

3 Stir $1\frac{1}{2}$ Tbsp of the flour into the casserole, then add the tomato paste. Stir for 1–2 minutes, then pour in the orange juice and stock and bring to the boil, stirring.

4 Return the meat to the casserole, add the bay leaves and seasoning to taste and stir well to mix. Cover and cook in the oven at 350°F for $1\frac{1}{2}$ hours or until the lamb is just tender. Leave in a cool place overnight.

5 *To serve* (1 hour 25 minutes): Make the dumplings. Sift the remaining flour and a pinch of salt on to a sheet of waxed paper. Put the butter in a medium saucepan, add the water and heat gently until the butter has melted.

6 Bring the water to a rolling boil and tip in the flour and salt all at once.

7 Immediately take the pan off the heat and beat vigorously until the mixture forms a ball and leaves the sides of the pan clean.

8 Turn the ball into a bowl and leave to cool for 1–2 minutes, then beat in the eggs a little at a time. The finished batter should be quite stiff.

9 Beat the orange rind and parsley into the batter. Remove the bay leaves from the casserole, then pipe or spoon 8 pastry balls on top.

10 Bake uncovered in the oven at 400°F for about 1 hour until the dumplings are risen and golden brown. Serve hot, straight from the casserole, garnished with parsley and orange shreds.

Menu Suggestion
Serve for an informal dinner party with a seasonal green vegetable such as broccoli, Brussels sprouts or green beans.

MARINATED LAMB CHOPS

1.45* | $ $ | 714 cals

* plus 12 hours marinating and 1 hour cooling

Serves 6

5 lb rack of lamb

2 cups dry white wine

1 cup vegetable oil

4 Tbsp chopped fresh rosemary or 4 tsp dried

1 tsp salt

freshly ground pepper

1 large garlic clove, crushed

1½ lb pickling onions

2 Tbsp brown sugar

2 Tbsp red wine

2 Tbsp tomato paste

1 *To prepare* (1 hour 45 minutes): Trim away any excess fat, and remove the flesh between each cutlet bone. Place the meat in a glass or china dish.

2 Mix the white wine, 8 Tbsp oil, rosemary, seasoning and crushed garlic together and pour over the meat. Cover and marinate for 12 hours, turning once.

3 While the meat is marinating, heat the remaining vegetable oil in a large frying pan, add the onions with the sugar and stir well. Cook over moderate heat for about 15 minutes until well-browned, shaking the pan occasionally.

4 Add the red wine and tomato paste and bring to the boil. Lower the heat and cook gently, uncovered, for 5–10 minutes until the onions are glazed. Remove from the heat, cool and chill.

5 Lift the meat out of the marinade and place on a rack standing over a roasting tin.

6 Cook in the oven at 350°F for about 1½ hours or until the meat is tender, basting occasionally.

7 While still warm, divide the meat into chops and spoon over the marinade. Baste and turn from time to time until cold, about 1 hour. Cover and leave in a cool place until serving time.

8 *To serve*: Arrange the chops on a serving plate and garnish with the onions. Serve chilled.

Menu Suggestion
Serve this as a main course for a dinner party. Start with Iced Zucchini Soup (page 27); finish with Pommes Bristol (page 73).

BEEF AND CHESTNUT CASSEROLE

2.45* ✳* 763 cals

* plus overnight cooling; freeze at the
end of step 4

Serves 4

3 Tbsp vegetable oil

2½ lb chuck steak, trimmed of fat
and cubed

1 medium onion, sliced

1 garlic clove, crushed

2 Tbsp wholewheat flour

1¼ cups hard cider or light beer

1¼ cups beef stock

2 Tbsp ketchup

1 tsp dried mixed herbs

salt and freshly ground pepper

15½ oz can whole chestnuts,
drained

2 Tbsp chopped fresh parsley,
to garnish

1 *To prepare* (2 hours
25 minutes): Heat the oil in a
large flameproof casserole, add the
beef in batches and fry over brisk
heat until browned on all sides.
Remove with a slotted spoon and
set aside.

2 Add the onion and garlic to
the casserole, lower the heat
and fry gently for 5 minutes until
soft but not colored.

3 Return the meat to the
casserole and stir in the flour.
Cook, stirring, for 1–2 minutes,
then stir in the cider or beer, stock
and ketchup. Bring slowly to the
boil, then add the herbs and
seasoning to taste.

4 Cover the casserole and cook
in the oven at 325°F for 2
hours or until the beef is tender.
Leave in a cool place overnight.

5 *To serve* (20 minutes): Reheat
the casserole on top of the
stove until bubbling, then add the
chestnuts and heat through for a
further 10 minutes. Taste and
adjust seasoning and sprinkle with
the parsley before serving.

Menu Suggestion
This is a hearty casserole, suitable
for a winter dinner party. Start
the meal with Smoked Trout
Mousse in Lemon Shells (page 14)
and finish with Coffee Bavarian
Cream (page 77) or Baked Rum
and Raisin Cheesecake (page 68).

BEEF AND CHESTNUT CASSEROLE

Cans of whole chestnuts are
available at most large supermarkets and delicatessens,
imported from France. They are
very convenient to use and have
a good flavor. Their texture is
rather soft, however, due to the
canning process. If you prefer
crunchier chestnuts, then fresh
chestnuts can be used, but it is
best to cook them beforehand and
add them to the casserole just to
heat through; otherwise you run
the risk of overcooking them. To
cook fresh chestnuts, first make a

small cut in the rounded part of
each shell with the point of a
small sharp knife. Put the
chestnuts in a saucepan and
cover with cold water. Bring
to the boil and simmer for 10
minutes, then drain. While the
chestnuts are still warm, peel off
both the outer shells and the
inner skins.

Cook the chestnuts in stock or
water to cover for about 20
minutes until tender, then drain
before use.

BITKIS

2.00*	$	637 cals

* plus overnight soaking and 2–3 hours cooling

Serves 6

2 cups rolled oats

1¼ cups milk

2 medium onions, roughly chopped

2 lb lean ground beef

salt and freshly ground pepper

3 tsp caraway seeds (optional)

5 Tbsp seasoned flour*

4 Tbsp vegetable oil

2 Tbsp butter

3 Tbsp flour

2 cups beef or chicken stock

2 Tbsp tomato paste

1¼ cups sour cream

parsley sprigs, to garnish

* Flour seasoned with salt, pepper and paprika

1 To prepare (40 minutes): Soak the oats in the milk overnight. Squeeze out excess milk and mix the oats with the onions, ground beef and seasoning to taste.

2 Put this mixture twice through a grinder or mix in a food processor until smooth. Beat in 2 tsp of the caraway seeds, if using.

3 Shape into 18 round flat cakes, or bitkis. Coat with seasoned flour.

4 Heat the oil in a large frying pan and brown the bitkis well. Place in a single layer in a large shallow ovenproof dish.

5 Melt the butter in a saucepan, add the flour and cook over low heat, stirring with a wooden spoon, for 2 minutes. Gradually blend in the stock, stirring after each addition to prevent lumps forming. Bring to the boil slowly, then simmer for 2–3 minutes, stirring. Stir in the tomato paste, sour cream and remaining caraway seeds, if using.

6 Pour the sauce over the bitkis and cool for 2–3 hours. Cover with foil and chill in the refrigerator until required.

7 To serve (1 hour 20 minutes): Bake in the oven at 350°F for about 1¼ hours or until the juices run clear when the bitkis are pierced. Garnish with parsley just before serving.

Menu Suggestion

Serve these Russian beef patties for a family meal with noodles and a mixed salad which includes grated or chopped beets.

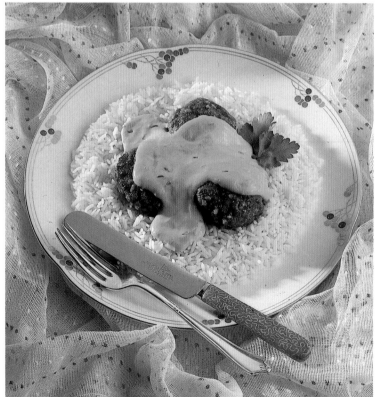

BEEF KABOBS WITH HORSERADISH RELISH

| 0.45 | $ | ✳ | 399 cals |

Serves 6

| 1½ lb lean ground beef |
| 2 cups grated onion |
| 9 Tbsp prepared horseradish |
| 3 Tbsp chopped fresh thyme |
| 3 cups fresh white breadcrumbs |
| salt and freshly ground pepper |
| 1 egg, beaten |
| flour, for coating |
| ⅔ cup plain yogurt |
| 8 Tbsp finely chopped fresh parsley |

1 To prepare (20 minutes): Place the ground beef in a large bowl and mix in the onion, 6 Tbsp of the horseradish, thyme, breadcrumbs and seasoning to taste.

2 Add enough egg to bind the mixture together and, with well-floured hands, shape into 18 even-sized sausages. Cover and chill in the refrigerator until required.

3 To serve (25 minutes): Thread the kabobs lengthwise onto 6 oiled skewers. Place under a pre-heated broiler and broil for about 20 minutes, turning frequently.

4 Meanwhile, mix the yogurt with the remaining horse-radish and parsley. Serve the kabobs hot, with the sauce handed separately.

Menu Suggestion
Serve Iced Zucchini Soup (page 27) for an appetizer and Mango Mousse for dessert (page 74).

BEEF KABOBS WITH HORSERADISH

Kabobs are very popular in Indian and Middle Eastern cooking, and this method of threading ground meat on skewers is a very common one. In India, such kabobs are cooked on the street, and passers-by stop to buy them and eat them as they are going along. A charcoal grill is used for cooking, which gives them such a wonderful aroma that they are hard to resist if you are hungry when walking by a kabob stall. If you have a barbecue, then cook the kabobs on it, and you will understand why!

PORK WITH CIDER AND CORIANDER

| 0.30 | $ $ | 418 cals |

Serves 4

1 lb pork fillet (tenderloin)
1 green pepper
2 stalks celery
1 large onion
2 Tbsp oil
4 Tbsp butter
1 Tbsp ground coriander
1 Tbsp flour
$\frac{2}{3}$ cup dry cider or light beer
$\frac{2}{3}$ cup chicken or vegetable stock
salt and freshly ground pepper

1 *To prepare* (15 minutes): Trim and slice the pork fillet into $\frac{1}{4}$ inch thick pieces. Place between sheets of plastic wrap and pound out thinly. Cover and chill until required.

2 Cut the pepper into rings, discarding the core and seeds. Slice the celery into $\frac{1}{4}$ inch pieces. Chop the onion. Cover the vegetables and chill in the refrigerator until required.

3 *To serve* (15 minutes): Heat the oil with half the butter in a large frying pan. Add the green pepper and celery and fry gently for 2–3 minutes. Lift out with a slotted spoon and keep warm on a serving plate.

4 Add the remaining butter, increase the heat to high, then add the pork, a few pieces at a time. Brown the pork on all sides, then remove from the pan.

5 Add the onion to the residual fat and fry until golden brown. Stir in the coriander and flour and cook for 1 minute. Add the cider or beer and stock and bring quickly to the boil, stirring constantly. Return the pork to the pan, add seasoning to taste and simmer for about 5 minutes. Serve hot, with the green pepper and celery.

Menu Suggestion

This dinner party main course would go well with Stuffed Mushrooms (page 17) to start and Pommes Bristol (page 73) to finish.

PORK WITH CIDER AND CORIANDER

Fillet or tenderloin of pork is a luxury cut of meat, but well worth the expense when you are entertaining, because you can rely on it being beautifully moist and tender, and there are no wasteful bones and fat. The fillet or tenderloin comes from beneath the center loin and the sirloin of the pig—the butcher detaches it and sells it separately rather than including it with loin chops. It is an excellent cut for quick pan-frying as in the recipe; it also makes a good roast if two fillets are tied together with a stuffing in between.

ORANGE GLAZED COUNTRY HAM

2.35*	$ $	490–613 cals

* plus 2–3 hours soaking and 3–4
hours cooling

Serves 8–10

4 lb smoked country ham butt
2 Tbsp Dijon mustard
3 Tbsp orange marmalade
¼ tsp ground allspice
⅓ cup brown sugar
salt and freshly ground pepper
1 orange
whole cloves
pickled walnuts and orange slices, to garnish

1 *To prepare* (2 hours
25 minutes): Cover the ham
with cold water and soak for 2–3
hours. Drain and calculate the
cooking time, allowing 25 minutes
per 1 lb.

2 Place the roast, skin side
down, in a large pan and cover
with cold water. Bring to the boil,
skim and reduce the heat. Cover
and simmer for half the cooking
time.

3 Drain the roast, wrap in foil,
then place in a roasting tin.
Continue to cook in the oven at
350°F for the rest of the calculated
time.

4 Make the glaze. Put the
mustard in a bowl with the
marmalade, allspice, sugar and
seasoning to taste. Mix well.

5 Remove the roast from the
oven and increase the oven
temperature to 400°F.

6 Unwrap the roast, strip off the
rind and slash the fat with a
sharp knife. Spread the fat with
half of the glaze. Place the joint in
a foil-lined roasting tin, return to
the oven and cook for 20 minutes.

7 Cut the orange into thin slices,
then halve them. Using cloves,
attach the orange pieces to the
joint. Brush with the remaining
glaze. Return to the oven for a
further 10 minutes, then cool for
3–4 hours. Chill in the refrigerator
until required.

8 *To serve* (10 minutes): Carve
into slices and garnish with
pickled walnuts and orange slices.

Menu Suggestion
This cold ham makes a spectacular
centerpiece for a buffet party
table. Serve with potato salad,
apple coleslaw, and beet and
orange salad. Marinated raw
mushrooms or Mushrooms in Red
Wine (page 54) would also go well.

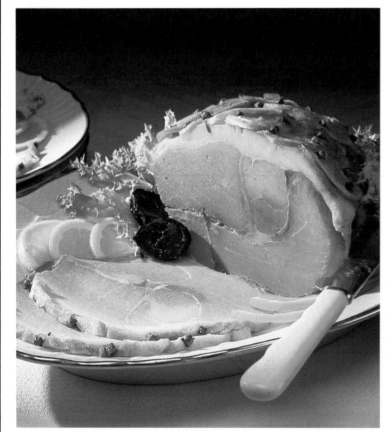

EGGPLANT STUFFED WITH HAM

| 1.45 | $ | 565 cals |

Serves 2

2 even-sized eggplants, about 1 lb
   total weight
vegetable oil
1 medium onion
4 oz cooked lean ham
4 Tbsp butter
1 garlic clove, crushed
2 Tbsp flour
2 tsp chopped fresh basil or ½ tsp
   dried
¾ cup fresh white breadcrumbs
1 tsp French mustard
1 tsp lemon juice
4 Tbsp light cream
salt and freshly ground pepper

1 To prepare (1 hour 15 minutes):
Cut the eggplants in half
lengthwise, then score the exposed
flesh on the cut sides.

2 Brush the eggplants with oil
and place, cut sides upper-
most, in an ovenproof dish. Add
4 Tbsp water, cover with foil or a
lid and bake in the oven at 375°F
for about 50 minutes until the
flesh is just tender. Do not
overcook.

3 With a sharp-edged teaspoon,
scoop out as much flesh from
the eggplants as possible, leaving
the shells intact. Chop the flesh.
Finely chop the onion and ham.

4 Melt half the butter in a saucepan, add the onion and fry
gently until soft. Add the garlic
and eggplant flesh and fry for 2–3
minutes.

5 Sprinkle over the flour and
basil; cook for 2–3 minutes,
stirring. Add the ham, all but
2 Tbsp of the breadcrumbs, the
mustard, lemon juice, cream and
seasoning to taste.

6 Fill the eggplant shells with
the stuffing. Top with the
reserved breadcrumbs and dot
with the remaining butter. Cover
and chill in the refrigerator until
required.

7 To serve (30 minutes): Bake in
the oven, uncovered, at 375°F
for about 30 minutes. Serve hot.

Menu Suggestion
Stuffed eggplants make a light
main course for an informal
supper party. Serve with a mixed
salad, French bread and a bottle of
full-bodied wine, and follow with
a selection of cheeses and grapes,
dates or figs.

SAUSAGE AND EGG PIE

| 1.30 | 🍴 | $ | 626–939 cals |

Serves 4–6

pie crust pastry (see page 156)
    made with 2 cups flour

3 eggs, hard-boiled

2 tsp prepared horseradish

8 oz sausage meat

2 eggs, beaten

$\frac{3}{4}$ cup light cream or milk

1 tsp chopped fresh sage or $\frac{1}{2}$ tsp
    dried

salt and freshly ground pepper

3 Reserve 2 tsp of the beaten eggs for glazing, then mix the remainder with the cream, sage and seasoning to taste. Pour into the tart case.

1 *To prepares* (30 minutes): Use two-thirds of the pastry to line an 8-inch tart ring placed on a baking sheet.

2 Shell the hard-boiled eggs and halve lengthwise. Mix the horseradish with the sausage meat, divide into 6 and mold over the white of each egg half. Place yolk side down in the tart case.

4 Cover with the remaining pastry, sealing the edges well. Decorate with pastry trimmings. Chill in the refrigerator until required.

5 *To serve* (1 hour): Glaze the pie with the reserved beaten eggs, then bake in the oven at 325°F for about 1 hour. Serve hot or cold.

Menu Suggestion
Sausage and Egg Pie makes a filling dish for a family supper. Serve hot with French beans tossed in melted herb butter. For a picnic or summer meal in the garden, serve the pie cold with a selection of salads.

SAUSAGE AND EGG PIE
This pie makes a filling family meal from everyday ingredients, yet shows you have gone to a little more trouble than simply giving them sausage and eggs! For best results, choose a good-quality sausage meat which is not too fatty. Some varieties, especially those that butchers make themselves, have herbs and spices added, which would give the filling a tasty flavor. Served cold, this pie is also excellent for picnics and box lunches.

CHICKEN POT PIES

3.00*	* *	847 cals

* plus cooling overnight; freeze without pastry glaze in step 10

Serves 4

3-lb chicken, giblets removed

1 lemon

few sprigs of fresh tarragon or ½ tsp dried

1 bay leaf

salt and freshly ground pepper

2 leeks, trimmed and sliced

2 large carrots, peeled and thinly sliced

6 oz button onions, topped and stemmed

3 Tbsp butter or margarine

6 oz button mushrooms, wiped and halved or sliced if large

3 Tbsp flour

4 Tbsp heavy cream

13 oz package frozen puff pastry, thawed

a little beaten egg, to glaze

1 To prepare (2 hours 15 minutes): Wash the chicken inside and out. Prick the lemon all over with a skewer, then place inside the chicken.

2 Put the chicken in a large saucepan with the tarragon, bay leaf and seasoning to taste. Add the giblets (except the liver), then pour in just enough water to cover the chicken and bring slowly to the boil. Lower the heat, half cover with a lid and simmer for 1¼ hours or until tender.

3 Add the leeks and carrots for the last 30 minutes of the cooking time. Remove the pan from the heat and leave the chicken and vegetables to cool in the liquid.

4 Remove the chicken from the cooking liquid. Cut the flesh from the bird, discarding all skin and bones. Dice the flesh into bite-sized pieces. Set aside.

5 Place the button onions in a bowl, pour in boiling water to cover and leave for 2–3 minutes. Drain and plunge into cold water, then remove the onions one at a time and peel off the skins with your fingers.

6 Melt the butter or margarine in a clean saucepan, add the onions and fry gently for 5 minutes until lightly colored.

7 Strain the cooking liquid from the chicken, measure and reserve 1¼ cups. Add the mushrooms to the onions, together with the leeks and carrots, discarding the tarragon sprigs, if used, and the bay leaf. Fry the vegetables gently for 1–2 minutes, then add the chicken pieces and fry for a few minutes more.

8 Mix the flour to a paste with the cream. Gradually blend in the measured cooking liquid, then pour into the pan of chicken and vegetables. Add seasoning to taste. Simmer, stirring, for 2–3 minutes, then turn into four 1½-cup ovenproof pie dishes. Cover and leave until completely cold, overnight if convenient.

9 To serve (45 minutes): Roll out the pastry on a floured surface and cut out four circles or ovals to make lids. Cut four strips of pastry long enough to go around the rims of the dishes.

10 Dampen the rims of the pie dishes, then place the strips of pastry around them. Dampen the pastry strips, then place the circles of pastry on top. Press firmly to seal, then knock up and flute. Make a hole in the center of each pie and decorate with pastry trimmings if desired. Glaze with beaten egg.

11 Bake the pies in the oven at 400°F for 25 minutes or until the pastry is golden brown and the filling heated through. Serve hot.

Menu Suggestion

These individual pies are perfect for an informal supper party, served simply with a tossed mixed salad and beer or wine. Follow with a selection of different cheeses and fresh fruit.

CHICKEN AND RED CURRANT CURRY

1.30* ✳ 441 cals

* plus 2–3 hours cooling

Serves 4

4 chicken leg joints

3 large onions, roughly chopped

1 inch piece fresh ginger, peeled and finely chopped

2 garlic cloves, crushed

2 Tbsp vegetable oil

2 tsp ground cumin

2 tsp ground coriander

1 tsp chili powder

½ tsp ground turmeric

2 Tbsp lemon juice

1 cup red currant jelly

1 cup chicken stock

salt and freshly ground pepper

2 bay leaves

coriander sprigs, to garnish

1 *To prepare* (1 hour 10 minutes): Cut the chicken legs into thighs and drumsticks; remove skin and fat.

2 In a blender or food processor, work the onions, ginger and garlic together until fairly smooth.

3 Heat the oil in large heavy-based pan, add the onion paste and fry gently until golden. Add the chicken pieces and fry until golden on all sides.

4 Add the cumin, coriander, chili, turmeric and lemon juice. Cook for 5 minutes until the chicken pieces are evenly coated with spices, then stir in the red currant jelly, stock and seasoning to taste. Bring to the boil, add the bay leaves, cover and simmer for 45–50 minutes or until the chicken is tender.

5 Remove from the heat, leave to cool for 2–3 hours, then cover and chill in the refrigerator until required.

6 *To serve* (20 minutes): Bring to the boil on top of the cooker, then lower the heat and simmer gently for 10–15 minutes to heat through. Taste and adjust seasoning and garnish with coriander just before serving.

Menu Suggestion

Serve as part of an Indian-style meal with Curried Parsnip and Orange Soup (page 26) to start and Mango Mousse (page 74) to follow. The curry itself is best served with boiled white rice and side dishes of sliced banana and coconut, yogurt and cucumber, mango chutney and lime pickle.

CHICKEN AND RED CURRANT CURRY

If you have time, the chicken in this recipe would benefit from being marinated in the onion, ginger and garlic paste. After skinning the chicken, make a few slashes in the flesh with the tip of a sharp knife, then place in a bowl and spread with the paste. If you like, you can add the juice of 1 lime or ½ a lemon. Leave for at least 1 hour, or overnight in the refrigerator if possible. Fry the paste and chicken together in step 3, then continue as in the recipe above.

CHICKEN AND CAPER CROQUETTES

| 1.00* | 🍴 | $ | 302 cals |

* plus 30 minutes cooling and several hours chilling

Makes 12

3 lb chicken, poached
½ cup butter
1 cup flour
2½ cups milk
2 Tbsp chopped fresh tarragon or 2 tsp dried
1 Tbsp chopped fresh parsley
2 Tbsp chopped capers
salt and freshly ground pepper
2 eggs, beaten
¾ cup fresh white breadcrumbs
¼ cup chopped almonds
vegetable oil, for frying

1 *To prepare* (45 minutes): Remove the flesh from the cold chicken and dice roughly.

2 Melt the butter in a saucepan, add the flour and cook over low heat, stirring with a wooden spoon, for 2 minutes. Gradually blend in the milk, stirring after each addition to prevent lumps forming. Bring to the boil slowly, then simmer for at least 10 minutes, until very thick. Stir in the tarragon, parsley and capers. Season well and leave to cool for 30 minutes.

3 Stir in the chicken and spread the mixture out on a large flat plate. Chill in the refrigerator for several hours.

4 Divide the mixture into 12 equal sections. Shape each into a croquette 2½ inches long, using floured hands.

5 Brush each croquette evenly with beaten egg. Mix the breadcrumbs and almonds together and use to coat the croquettes. Pat well in, to coat thoroughly and evenly. Chill in the refrigerator until required.

6 *To serve* (15 minutes): Deep fry in oil at 350°F for 4–5 minutes or shallow fry for about 6–7 minutes until golden brown. Drain well on absorbent paper before serving.

Menu Suggestion
These croquettes make a tasty everyday main course for the family. Serve with a mixed salad tossed in lots of blue cheese dressing, or with coleslaw. Children will probably enjoy them best with French fries.

TURKEY CASSEROLE WITH RED WINE

| 3.20* | ✳ | 434–495 cals |

* plus 2–3 hours cooling

Serves 4

2 Tbsp butter

2 Tbsp vegetable oil

1–1½ lb turkey casserole meat

4 oz lean streaky bacon, rinded and diced

2 Tbsp flour

good pinch of dried thyme

1 bay leaf

⅔ cup red wine

1¼ cups water (or unseasoned stock)

salt and freshly ground pepper

12 small onions or shallots, peeled

chopped fresh parsley and pastry crescents or croûtons, to serve

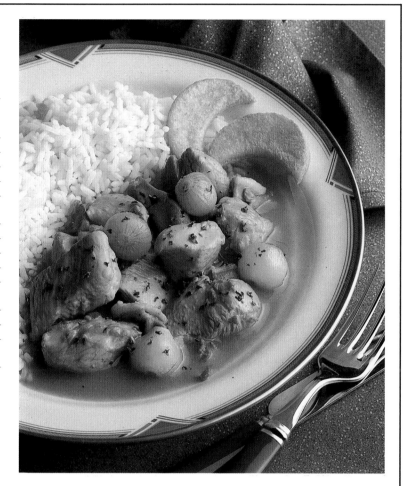

1 *To prepare* (2 hours 30 minutes): Melt half the butter with half the oil in a large frying pan. When foaming, add the turkey meat and brown well. Remove with a slotted spoon and place in a casserole.

2 Add the bacon to the frying pan and fry until beginning to brown. Remove the bacon with a slotted spoon and add to the turkey.

3 Stir the flour, thyme and bay leaf into the fat left in the frying pan and cook gently for a few minutes. Slowly stir in the red wine, water and seasoning to taste. Bring to the boil, stirring, then pour over the turkey.

4 Cover the casserole tightly and cook in the oven at 300°F for about 2 hours.

5 Thirty minutes before the end of the cooking time, melt the remaining butter and oil in a frying pan. Add the onions and cook slowly until golden brown and tender. Add the onions to the casserole, cool for 2–3 hours, then chill in the refrigerator until required.

6 *To serve* (20–50 minutes): Place the casserole on top of the cooker, slowly bring to the boil, then lower the heat and simmer for 20 minutes.

7 Alternatively, reheat in the oven at 425°F for 30 minutes or until boiling, then at 300°F for 20 minutes. Garnish with parsley and pastry crescents or croûtons and serve hot.

Menu Suggestion
Serve for a dinner party with Stuffed Mushrooms (page 17) to start and Sherried Apricot Trifle (page 70) to finish.

TURKEY CASSEROLE WITH RED WINE

Small pickling onions and shallots are not always easy to obtain all year round, yet they do look attractive whole in this casserole. If you are unable to get them, use 2 medium onions, peeled and chopped, and fry them with the diced bacon in step 2 of the recipe. To improve the appearance of the finished dish, add 4–6 oz whole button mushrooms in step 5 instead of the whole onions.

SUMMER FISH HOT POT

1.10*	$	459 cals

* plus 30 minutes cooling

Serves 4

4 stalks of celery, washed and
    trimmed

4 Tbsp butter

$\frac{1}{3}$ cup flour

2 cups milk

salt and freshly ground pepper

$1\frac{1}{2}$ lb firm white fish fillets
    (cod, haddock or monkfish)

1 bulb Florence fennel, untrimmed

4 Tbsp chopped parsley

2 tsp lemon juice

1 lb new potatoes, boiled

chopped fresh parsley, to garnish

1 To prepare (20 minutes): Slice
the celery finely. Melt
the butter in a flameproof
casserole, add the celery and cook
gently for 5 minutes until soft.
Add the flour and cook over low
heat, stirring with a wooden
spoon, for 2 minutes. Remove
from the heat and gradually blend
in the milk, stirring after each
addition to prevent lumps
forming. Bring to the boil slowly,
then simmer for 2–3 minutes,
stirring. Add seasoning to taste
and remove from the heat.

2 Place the fish in a saucepan
and just cover with water.
Bring to the boil, remove from the
heat and drain. Cut into fork-size
pieces, discarding the skin and any
bones.

3 Trim the fennel and cut into
thin slices. Blanch in boiling
salted water for 2 minutes and
drain.

4 Add the fennel, parsley and
lemon juice to the sauce; mix
well. Stir in the fish, taking care
not to break up the flesh; cool for
30 minutes.

5 Slice the cooked potatoes and
arrange on top of the fish.
Cover the dish with buttered foil
and chill in the refrigerator until
required.

6 To serve (50 minutes): Bake in
the oven, with foil covering, at
350°F for about 50 minutes or
until the fish is cooked. Sprinkle
with chopped parsley before
serving.

Menu Suggestion
This Mediterranean style fish stew
contains fennel and potatoes, and
so does not need a vegetable
accompaniment. Serve for an
informal meal with crusty fresh
bread or bread rolls, and a
bottle of chilled dry white wine.

CREAMED SEAFOOD VOL-AU-VENTS

| 0.55* | ✳* | 684 cals |

* plus cooling and overnight chilling of filling; freeze filling at the end of step 5

Serves 4

1 lb monkfish or haddock fillets

1 bay leaf

few black peppercorns

few parsley sprigs

1 slice of onion

1¼ cups milk

2 Tbsp butter or margarine

3 Tbsp flour

⅔ cup light cream

1 cup finely grated Gruyère cheese

¼ tsp ground mace or grated nutmeg

salt and freshly ground pepper

8 oz shrimp, defrosted and thoroughly dried if frozen

16 medium 2½–3 inch frozen vol-au-vent cases

beaten egg, to glaze

1 *To prepare* (30 minutes): Put the monkfish or haddock in a saucepan with the bay leaf, peppercorns, parsley and onion. Pour over the milk, then bring to the boil. Cover tightly, remove from the heat and leave until cold.

2 Remove the fish from the cooking liquid and reserve. Flake the flesh of the fish roughly, discarding any skin and or bones. Set aside.

3 Melt the butter or margarine in a heavy-based saucepan. Sprinkle in the flour and cook, stirring, for 1–2 minutes.

4 Remove from the heat and stir in the strained cooking liquid a little at a time, whisking vigorously until smooth. Simmer gently for 2 minutes, then add the cream and ¾ cup of the Gruyère cheese. Stir over very low heat until the cheese has melted.

5 Turn the sauce into a bowl and add the mace or nutmeg and seasoning to taste. Gently fold in the flaked white fish and the shrimp. Cover the surface of the sauce closely with plastic wrap, leave until cold, then chill overnight.

6 *To serve* (25 minutes): Place the frozen vol-au-vent cases on a dampened baking sheet and brush the rims carefully with beaten egg. Bake in the oven at 425°F for about 15 minutes or according to package instructions.

7 Meanwhile reheat the filling gently in a heavy-based saucepan until hot and bubbling. Taste and adjust seasoning.

8 Remove the soft centers from the vol-au-vent cases, spoon in the filling, then replace the crisp tops. Serve piping hot.

Menu Suggestion
These vol-au-vents are rather special. Serve them as an impressive dinner party main course with a green vegetable such as snow peas, or zucchini tossed in melted butter and the finely grated rind and juice of a lime. Start the meal with Terrine of Chicken with Wine (page 9) and finish with Iced Orange Sabayon (page 79).

CREAMED SEAFOOD VOL-AU-VENTS
Frozen uncooked vol-au-vent cases, available at most super-markets, are an absolute boon to the busy cook, because you can quite literally take them from the package and pop them in the oven—and you get perfectly shaped and beautifully risen vol-au-vents every time.

Vegetables and Salads

Most vegetable and salad dishes need to be prepared just before serving to retain maximum crispness and freshness, but this doesn't mean that you have to leave everything to the last minute. Plan to do at least one vegetable or salad dish in advance—this is especially important when entertaining, as it will give you more time to enjoy the company of your guests.

GRUYÈRE POTATOES

| 2.35* | $ | ✳ | 303 cals |

Serves 6

2 lb potatoes
2 Tbsp butter
1 cup grated Gruyère cheese
freshly grated nutmeg
salt and freshly ground pepper
2½ cups milk

1 *To prepare* (1 hour 50 minutes): Peel the potatoes, then slice thinly. (Do not soak them in cold water.)

2 Use a little of the butter to lightly grease a 6-cup shallow ovenproof dish.

3 Layer the potatoes and most of the cheese in the dish. Add a generous grating of nutmeg, and seasoning to taste.

4 Top with cheese and then pour over the milk, which should just cover the potatoes.

5 Dot the surface with the remaining butter. Cover with foil and bake in the oven at 350°F for about 1½ hours or until the potatoes are quite tender and most of the milk has been absorbed. Cool, cover with clean foil and chill in the refrigerator until required.

6 *To serve* (45 minutes): Uncover and bake in the oven at 350°F for 45 minutes until the top is golden brown. Serve hot.

Menu Suggestion
Gruyère potatoes are a special occasion dish. Serve them for a dinner party with a main course of roast meat or a casserole, which can be cooked in the oven at the same time.

GRUYÈRE POTATOES
Gruyère potatoes are a variation of the famous French potato dish called *gratin dauphinois*, in which the potatoes are cooked in cream, rather than milk as suggested here. For a special occasion, you can use cream, or a combination of cream and milk, which will be less rich — and less expensive. Some French cooks add finely chopped onion and crushed garlic to this dish, which give it a good flavor.

Cheddar cheese can be used for an everyday occasion, but it does not give such a good melt-in-the-mouth texture as Gruyère. When preparing the potatoes for baked dishes such as this one, it is very important to slice them as thin as possible. For a simpler, less rich dish, try Layered French-Style Potatoes (page 138), which has a mustardy flavor.

MUSHROOMS IN RED WINE

1.05* | 131 cals

* plus about 4 hours marinating and overnight chilling

Serves 4

12 oz small button mushrooms

1¼ cups red wine

1 Tbsp crushed coriander seeds

salt and freshly ground pepper

2 Tbsp olive oil

1 small onion, finely chopped

1 garlic clove, crushed

1 Tbsp tomato paste

2 Tbsp chopped fresh coriander
   or continental parsley

8 lettuce leaves, to serve

1 To prepare (30 minutes): Wipe the mushrooms with a damp cloth; leave them whole if they are very small, otherwise halve them or cut them into even slices.

2 Put the mushrooms in a bowl with the red wine, coriander seeds and seasoning to taste. Cover and leave to marinate for about 4 hours.

3 Heat the olive oil in a heavy-based frying pan. Add the onion and fry gently for 5 minutes until soft but not colored. Add the garlic and tomato paste and fry for 2 minutes more.

4 Drain the marinade from the mushrooms and reserve. Add the mushrooms to the frying pan, increase the heat and fry, stirring, for 2 minutes until the juices run.

5 Pour the reserved marinade into the pan and bring to boiling point. Remove from the heat, turn into a bowl and leave until cold. Cover with plastic wrap and chill in the refrigerator overnight.

6 To serve (35 minutes): Stir the coriander or parsley into the mushrooms. Leave to stand at room temperature for about 30 minutes, then taste and adjust seasoning. Place 2 lettuce leaves in each of 4 individual dishes and spoon the mushrooms on them. Serve immediately or the lettuce will become limp.

Menu Suggestion

With their pungent sauce, these mushrooms make a tasty side dish to serve with cold meats, especially pork and ham. They are also good served as a starter, with crusty French bread and butter.

MUSHROOMS IN RED WINE

Do you know how good mushrooms are for you? They contain more protein per 4 oz than most other vegetables, and are also rich in vitamins B1, B2 and B6, and in the minerals potassium, copper and phosphorus. With no cholesterol and no carbohydrates, and only 7 calories per 4 oz, they're also good for dieters, especially when eaten raw. To obtain the full food value from cultivated mushrooms, don't wash or peel them; wipe with a damp cloth.

WATERCRESS AND OATMEAL CROQUETTES

1.05* ☐ $ ✳ 425 cals

* plus at least 30 minutes chilling

Serves 4

1½ lb mealy potatoes
1 Tbsp butter, softened
1 bunch watercress
2 eggs
salt and freshly ground pepper
1 Tbsp flour
¾ cup fresh breadcrumbs
½ cup medium oatmeal
vegetable oil, for deep frying

1 *To prepare* (50 minutes): Scrub the potatoes and boil in their skins until tender; about 20 minutes. Drain well.

2 Peel the potatoes, then sieve them into a bowl or mash *well*. Beat in the butter.

3 Wash, drain and finely chop the watercress. Add to the bowl with 1 egg and seasoning to taste; mix well.

4 Mold the potato mixture into 12 cork-shaped pieces. Coat each croquette lightly in flour.

5 Break the remaining egg on to a plate; beat lightly. Combine the breadcrumbs and oatmeal on another plate.

6 Brush the croquettes with the beaten egg, then coat in the breadcrumb mixture, pressing it on firmly. Chill in the refrigerator for at least 30 minutes or until required.

7 *To serve* (15 minutes): Heat the oil in a deep fat fryer to 375°F. Deep fry the croquettes for about 4 minutes or until golden brown on all sides. Drain on absorbent paper before serving.

Menu Suggestion
These croquettes make an unusual, colorful alternative to potatoes, and go especially well with lamb and fish dishes.

SALSIFY AU GRATIN

0.45* | $ | ✳ | 316 cals

* plus 30 minutes cooling

Serves 4

1 lb salsify, trimmed and peeled

1¼ cups chicken stock

2 Tbsp butter

3 Tbsp flour

½ tsp mustard powder

6 oz mature Cheddar cheese, grated

salt and freshly ground pepper

¾ cup fresh breadcrumbs

1 *To prepare* (20 minutes): Cut the salsify into 1 inch lengths and place in a saucepan with the stock.

2 Bring to the boil, cover and simmer gently for 15–20 minutes until tender. Drain, reserving the stock, and place the salsify in an overproof dish.

3 Melt the butter in a saucepan, add the flour and mustard powder and cook over low heat, stirring with a wooden spoon, for 2 minutes. Remove the pan from the heat and gradually blend in the reserved stock, stirring after each addition to prevent lumps forming.

4 Bring to the boil slowly, then simmer for 2–3 minutes, stirring. Add half the cheese and seasoning to taste and pour over the salsify.

5 Mix the remaining cheese with the breadcrumbs and sprinkle over the dish. Cool for 30 minutes, cover and chill in the refrigerator until required.

6 *To serve* (25 minutes): Uncover and bake in the oven at 375°F for 20–25 minutes until the top is golden brown. Serve hot.

Menu Suggestion

Hot, cheesy and bubbling, this unusual vegetable dish taste delicious with plain roast meats, and can be cooked in the oven at the same time. Try it with the Sunday roast for a change.

SALSIFY AU GRATIN

Salsify is an inexpensive winter vegetable. It looks rather like a long, thin parsnip, and has a soft, white flesh. Years ago it used to be nicknamed the "oyster vegetable," because its flavor was thought to be similar to that of oysters. Try coating chunks of salsify in batter after parboiling, then deep-frying them as a tasty alternative to chips.

CHILI POTATO SALAD

| 0.35* | $ | 448 cals |

* plus 2 hours chilling

Serves 6

2 lb even-sized new potatoes
1 medium green pepper
1 medium red pepper
1 cup vegetable oil
5 Tbsp garlic vinegar
1 Tbsp chili powder
salt and freshly ground pepper
1 medium onion, chopped
2 Tbsp sesame seeds
fresh coriander, to garnish

1 To prepare (30 minutes): Scrub the potatoes and boil in their skins until tender; about 20 minutes. Drain well.

2 Meanwhile, halve, seed and chop the peppers. Blanch them in boiling water for 1–2 minutes. Drain well.

3 In a large bowl, whisk together the oil, vinegar, chili seasoning and salt and pepper to taste.

4 Halve the potatoes if they are large, but do not peel them. While still hot, stir into the dressing with the onion and peppers. Cool, cover and chill in the refrigerator for about 2 hours.

5 To serve (5 minutes): Toast the sesame seeds under the grill, leave to cool, then stir through the salad. Taste and adjust the seasoning before serving, garnished with fresh coriander.

Menu Suggestion
Serve this spicy potato salad with cold meats for lunch, or as a vegetable accompaniment to barbecued chicken or steak.

CAULIFLOWER, BEAN AND CAPER SALAD

2.40* | $ | 353 cals

* plus overnight soaking and 4 hours standing

Serves 4

¾ cup dried red kidney beans, soaked in cold water overnight

1 small onion, finely chopped

1–2 garlic cloves, crushed

3 Tbsp olive oil

1 Tbsp red wine vinegar

1 tsp French mustard

salt and freshly ground pepper

1 head cauliflower

4 Tbsp plain yogurt or sour cream

4 Tbsp mayonnaise

2 Tbsp roughly chopped capers

2 Tbsp chopped fresh parsley

1 To prepare (2 hours): Drain and rinse the kidney beans, then place in a pan with plenty of water. Bring to the boil and boil rapidly for 10 minutes. Lower the heat, half cover with a lid and simmer for 1½ hours or until the beans are tender.

2 Drain the beans, transfer to a bowl and immediately add the onion, garlic, olive oil, wine vinegar, mustard and seasoning to taste. Stir well to mix, then cover and leave for at least 4 hours to allow the dressing to flavor the beans.

3 To serve (40 minutes): Divide the cauliflower into small sprigs, cutting away all tough stalks. Wash the florets thoroughly under cold running water, then blanch in boiling water for 1 minute only. Drain thoroughly.

4 Add the cauliflower florets to the bean salad with the yogurt or sour cream, mayonnaise, capers and parsley. Mix well and chill in the refrigerator for 30 minutes before serving.

Menu Suggestion
This colorful salad makes a delicious lunch dish served with crusty wholewheat bread, and the combination of beans and grain provides first-class protein, thus making it a most nutritious meal.

CAULIFLOWER, BEAN AND CAPER SALAD
If you are short of time for making this salad, you can of course use canned red kidney beans, but they will not absorb the flavor of the dressing so well.

ORIENTAL RICE RING

1.00*	565 cals

* plus at least 4 hours or overnight chilling

Serves 4

1 cup brown rice

salt and freshly ground pepper

¼ cup creamed coconut

7 Tbsp vegetable oil

1 Tbsp soy sauce

1 Tbsp wine vinegar

1 tsp clear honey

2 carrots

1 red pepper

¾ cup bean sprouts

¼ cup unsalted peanuts, chopped

1 Tbsp lemon juice

1 To prepare (40 minutes): Cook the brown rice in plenty of boiling salted water until tender: about 30 minutes or according to package instructions.

2 Meanwhile, grate or break up the creamed coconut into a bowl. Add 4 Tbsp of the oil, the soy sauce, vinegar and honey and beat well to mix.

3 Drain the rice well and tip into the bowl of dressing. Stir quickly to mix, add seasoning to taste, then spoon into a lightly oiled 4-cup ring mold. Press down well, cover and chill in the refrigerator for at least 4 hours, or overnight if more convenient.

4 To serve (20 minutes): Prepare the vegetables. Scrape the carrots, then grate them finely. Cut the red pepper in half, remove the core and seeds, then cut the flesh into thin strips.

5 Combine the carrots, red pepper, bean sprouts and peanuts with the remaining oil and the lemon juice. Add seasoning to taste.

6 Turn the rice ring out on to a flat serving plate. Pile the salad in the center just before serving.

Menu Suggestion

This attractive salad makes a most nutritious lunch served with crusty rolls, cheese and a green salad.

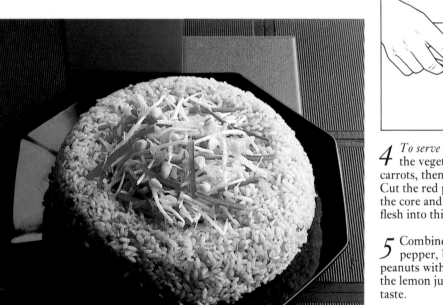

CUCUMBER SALAD

| 1.10* | 128 cals |

* plus 4 hours or overnight chilling

Serves 4

1 large cucumber
salt and freshly ground pepper
3 Tbsp white wine vinegar
3 Tbsp water
3 Tbsp sugar
½ tsp dillweed
⅔ cup sour cream
⅔ cup thick-set plain yogurt
2 Tbsp snipped chives

1 To prepare (1 hour): Using a cannelle knife or vegetable peeler, peel lengthwise strips off the cucumber. Slice the cucumber thinly into rings.

2 Put the cucumber slices in a colander, sprinkling each layer liberally with salt. Cover with a plate, place heavy weights on top, then leave for 30 minutes.

3 Meanwhile make the dressing. Put the vinegar, water and sugar in a saucepan and heat gently. Boil for 1 minute, remove from the heat and leave to cool.

4 Rinse the cucumber slices quickly under cold running water, then pat dry; place in a bowl. Stir the dill into the dressing with plenty of pepper, then pour over the cucumber. Cover and chill for 4 hours or overnight, turning the slices occasionally.

5 To serve (10 minutes): Mix the sour cream and yogurt with the chives; season to taste. Arrange the cucumber on a serving plate; spoon the dressing in the center. Serve chilled.

Menu Suggestion
Cucumber Salad is popular in Scandinavian countries, where it is usually served with fish.

LEMON BEAN SALAD

| 2.00* | 312 cals |

* plus overnight soaking and 4 hours standing

Serves 4

½ cup green flageolet beans (see box), soaked in cold water overnight

6 Tbsp olive oil

finely grated rind and juice of 1 lemon

1–2 garlic cloves, crushed

salt and freshly ground pepper

2 oz black olives

2 Tbsp chopped mixed fresh herbs, e.g. basil, marjoram, lemon balm, chives

4 large firm tomatoes

about ¼ tsp sugar

1 To prepare (1 hour 30 minutes): Drain and rinse the beans, then place in a pan with plenty of water. Bring to the boil, then lower the heat, half cover with a lid and simmer for about 1 hour until tender.

2 Drain the beans, transfer to a bowl and immediately add the oil, lemon rind and juice, garlic and seasoning to taste. Stir well to mix, then cover and leave for at least 4 hours to allow the dressing to flavor the beans.

3 To serve (30 minutes): Pit the olives, then chop roughly. Add to the salad with the herbs, then taste and adjust seasoning.

4 Peel the tomatoes. Put them in a bowl, pour over boiling water and leave for 2 minutes. Drain, then plunge into a bowl of cold water. Remove the tomatoes one at a time and peel off the skin with your fingers.

5 Slice the tomatoes thinly, then arrange on 4 serving plates. Sprinkle with sugar and seasoning to taste. Pile the bean salad on top of each plate. Serve chilled.

Menu Suggestion

Fresh and tangy, this summer salad can be served on its own as a starter or light lunch dish, or as an accompaniment to cold meats, especially cold roast chicken or turkey.

LEMON BEAN SALAD

Green flageolet beans are a very pretty, delicate light green in color. They are haricot beans which have been removed from their pods when very young and tender, and they get their name from the French word for flute, which they are said to resemble in shape. Some large supermarkets stock green flageolets, but health food shops probably have the fastest turnover. It is important that they have not been stored for too long because, like all dried beans, they become stale and will not soften, no matter how long you cook them.

Desserts

The last course of any meal is the first one to think of when preparing in advance. Most desserts are delicious served cold, but you should also remember that by the time you've finished eating the main course, you simply won't feel like leaving the table to start cooking all over again. How much more sensible it is to have the dessert ready to carry to the table—and collect all the compliments.

RASPBERRY ALMOND TART

1.40* ⬚ ✳ 568 cals

* plus 1 hour cooling

Serves 8

2 cups all-purpose flour
1 cup butter or margarine
⅔ cup light brown sugar
2 eggs, separated
1 cup self-rising flour
¾ cup ground almonds
4 Tbsp milk
8 oz raspberries
⅔ cup heavy cream, to serve

1 *To prepare* (1 hour 25 minutes): Sift the all-purpose flour into a bowl. Rub in half the fat until the mixture resembles fine bread-crumbs. Bind to a firm dough with 2–4 Tbsp ice water.

2 Knead the dough lightly on a floured surface, then roll out and use to line a 10 inch loose-based fluted tart tin.

3 Bake blind in the oven at 400°F for 15–20 minutes until set but not browned.

4 Meanwhile beat the remaining fat with the sugar until light and fluffy. Gradually beat in the egg yolks. Gently stir in the self-rising flour, ground almonds and milk. Whisk the egg whites until stiff, then fold into the mixture.

5 Spoon the cake mixture into the baked tart case and level the surface. Sprinkle over the raspberries, reserving a few for decoration.

6 Bake in the oven at 350°F for about 35 minutes or until the tart is golden brown and firm to the touch. Cool completely — about 1 hour.

7 *To serve* (15 minutes): Whip the cream until thick, then use to decorate the tart with the reserved raspberries. Cut the tart into large wedges.

Menu Suggestion
This pretty dessert is good for a dinner party because it can be made completely the day before. Serve Chilled Ratatouille (page 22) to start, and Pork with Cider and Coriander (page 36) for the main course.

BAKED RUM AND RAISIN CHEESECAKE

1.25* $\square$ $ $ ✳ 452 cals

* plus 1 hour cooling

Serves 8

¾ **cup raisins**

5 Tbsp dark rum

2 cups self-rising flour

6 Tbsp butter

rind of 1 lemon

⅔ **cup sour cream**

4 oz cottage cheese

4 oz cream cheese

2 eggs, separated

⅓ **cup sugar**

⅔ **cup heavy cream**

1 Tbsp confectioners sugar,
    to decorate

1 To prepare (1 hour 20 minutes): Put the raisins and rum in a saucepan and bring to the boil. Turn off the heat and leave to cool for 15 minutes.

2 Meanwhile, sift the flour into a bowl. Rub in the butter.

3 Grate in the lemon rind, using the finest side of the grater. Bind to a smooth dough with the sour cream, then use to line a greased 10 inch tart dish.

4 In a bowl, beat together the cottage and cream cheeses. Stir in the rum and raisins.

5 In a separate bowl, whisk the egg yolks and sugar until pale and fluffy. Whisk in the cream, and continue whisking until the mixture is the consistency of lightly whipped cream. Fold into the cheese, rum and raisin mixture.

6 Whisk the egg whites until stiff and fold into the mixture. Pour it into the prepared pastry case and bake in the oven at 325°F for about 45 minutes. Turn off the heat and leave to cool in the oven for 15 minutes. Remove from the oven and cool for a further 45 minutes.

7 To serve (5 minutes): Cut into slices and dust with confectioners sugar.

Menu Suggestion

Serve this traditional, rich cheesecake after a light main course such as grilled steak, chops or Marinated Lamb Chops (page 30).

FRUIT AND NUT CRUMBLE

| 1.05 | $ | ✳* | 410 cals |

* freeze at the end of step 4

Serves 4

¾ cup wholewheat flour

pinch of salt

4 Tbsp butter or margarine

⅔ cup light brown sugar

¼ cup walnuts, finely chopped

3 cooking pears

1 large cooking apple

2 Tbsp red currant jelly

finely grated rind and juice of
1 lemon

1 To prepare (25 minutes): Mix the flour and salt in a bowl. Add the butter or margarine and rub in until the mixture resembles fine breadcrumbs. Stir in half the sugar and the walnuts. Set aside.

2 Peel and quarter the pears and apple. Remove the cores, then slice the flesh thinly.

3 In a bowl, mix the red currant jelly and the lemon rind and juice with the remaining sugar. Add the sliced fruit and fold gently to mix.

4 Turn the fruit into an oven-proof dish and sprinkle the crumble mixture over the top. Leave in a cool place or the refrigerator until ready to cook (overnight if convenient).

5 To serve (40 minutes): Bake in the oven at 350°F for 40 minutes or until the fruit feels soft when pierced with a skewer and the crumble topping is crisp and golden. Serve hot.

Menu Suggestion
This nutty pear and apple crumble is a filling family pudding. Serve with light cream, custard or ice cream.

SHERRIED APRICOT TRIFLE

1.00* | 573 cals

* plus cooling, setting and overnight chilling

Serves 8–10

14½ oz can apricot halves in natural juice

1 package orange- or tangerine-flavored gelatine

12 oz sponge cake

1¼ cups sherry

1 egg

2 egg yolks

3 Tbsp sugar

1 Tbsp cornstarch

2 cups milk

1¼ cups heavy cream

few strips of angelica and some glacé cherries, to decorate

1 To prepare (45 minutes): Drain the apricots and measure the juice. Make up the gelatine according to package instructions, using the apricot juice as part of the measured liquid. Leave in a cool place until cold and just beginning to set.

2 Meanwhile break up the cake with your fingers and place in the bottom of a glass serving dish. Pour over the sherry, place the apricots on top, reserving one for decoration, cover and leave to stand while making the custard.

3 Make the custard. Put the egg and egg yolks in a bowl with the sugar and whisk lightly together. Add the cornstarch and a few tablespoons of the milk and whisk again until combined.

4 Scald the milk in a heavy-based saucepan. Pour on to the egg mixture, stirring constantly, then return the custard to the rinsed-out pan. Cook over low to moderate heat, stirring all the time until the custard thickens and coats the back of the spoon. Pour immediately into a bowl, cover the surface of the custard closely with plastic wrap and leave until cold.

5 Pour the cold, setting gelatine over the apricots in the serving dish, spreading it evenly, then chill in the refrigerator until set.

6 Pour the cold custard over the gelatine, cover closely with plastic wrap and chill overnight.

7 To serve (15 minutes): Whip the cream until stiff, then swirl or pipe over the trifle leaving the center uncovered. Decorate with the remaining apricot, angelica "stalks," and glacé cherry "flowers." Serve chilled.

Menu Suggestion

A special occasion trifle, which can be served as a dessert for a buffet party, or as an afternoon treat.

SHERRIED APRICOT TRIFLE

Trifle is an old-fashioned English dish, traditionally served at Sunday tea time. Every English family has its own version, but the authentic English trifle which was so popular in Victorian days was a simple layered concoction of sponge cake soaked in sherry, almond-flavored macaroons, a rich egg custard and a topping of thickly whipped cream. Today's modern trifle with fruit and jelly would have been frowned upon by the Victorians.

The essence of making a good trifle lies in using a large quantity of sherry for soaking the cake base. It may seem extravagant when you are making it, but unless you use the amount specified in the recipe, you will not get the proper "boozy" flavor, which is vital to a really good special-occasion trifle like this.

POMMES BRISTOL

| 0.45* | 🍴 | $ | 303 cals |

* plus cooling and overnight chilling

Serves 4

1½ cups sugar

2 cups water

1 vanilla pod

4 crisp dessert apples (e.g. Granny
  Smiths or Greening)

2 small oranges

2 Tbsp orange-flavored liqueur
  (optional)

1 *To prepare* (40 minutes): Put
half the sugar in a heavy-based
saucepan with 1¼ cups of the water
and the vanilla pod. Heat gently
until the sugar has dissolved, then
simmer, without stirring, for 2–3
minutes.

2 Meanwhile, peel, quarter and
core the apples. Slice them
into the pan of syrup, remove
from the heat and cover with a lid.

3 Cut the rind and pith off the
oranges with a serrated knife,
working from top to bottom in a
spiral motion. Slice into thin
rounds or sections.

4 When the apples are cold,
remove them carefully from
the syrup with a slotted spoon.
Arrange them on a shallow serving
dish with the orange. Discard the
vanilla pod from the syrup and stir
in the liqueur, if using. Pour over
the apples and oranges, cover with
plastic wrap and chill in the
refrigerator overnight.

5 Put the remaining sugar and
water in the saucepan and heat
gently until the sugar has dissolved. Boil rapidly until the syrup
turns a rich caramel in color,
then pour immediately into a
greased shallow baking tin or tray.
Leave in a cold place overnight.

6 *To serve* (5 minutes): Crush
the caramel into small pieces
by hitting it with the end of a
rolling pin or a mallet. Sprinkle
over the apples and oranges and
serve immediately (the caramel
will soften if left on the fruit and
syrup for many minutes).

Menu Suggestion
Serve this fruity dessert after a
rich main course.

MANGO MOUSSE

1.00*	🍳	$ $	375 cals

* plus 15 minutes freezing or 1 hour chilling, and overnight refrigeration

Serves 6

2 ripe mangoes

3 eggs

1 egg yolk

$\frac{1}{4}$ cup sugar

finely grated rind of 1 orange

4 Tbsp orange-flavored liqueur or orange juice

1$\frac{1}{4}$ cups heavy cream

1 Tbsp unflavored gelatine

2 Tbsp lemon juice

2 Tbsp water

shreds of blanched orange rind, to decorate

1 To prepare (50 minutes): Cut a thick slice from either side of each central mango pit, keeping the knife close to the pit.

2 Scrape the mango flesh out of the skin and from around the pit. Place in a blender or food processor and work to a smooth purée, then rub through a nylon sieve into a bowl. Set aside.

3 With an electric mixer, beat the eggs, egg yolk and sugar in a separate bowl until thick and light in color. The beaters should leave a ribbon trail on the surface.

4 Add the mango purée. Whisk in the orange rind and the liqueur or orange juice to the egg mixture a little at a time, whisking well after each addition.

5 Whip half the cream until it is the same consistency as the mango mousse, then fold in.

6 Sprinkle the gelatine over the lemon juice and water in a small heatproof bowl. Leave for 5 minutes until spongy, then stand the bowl in a pan of gently simmering water to dissolve.

7 Pour the liquid gelatine into the mango mousse, stirring gently to distribute it evenly. Pour slowly into a chilled large serving dish. Freeze for 15 minutes or chill for 1 hour. Cover with plastic and chill overnight.

8 To serve (10 minutes): Whip the remaining cream until stiff, then use to pipe a shell border around the edge of the mousse. Sprinkle with orange shreds. Serve chilled.

Menu Suggestion

Mango Mousse is a very special dinner party dessert. Serve it after Beef Kabobs with Horseradish Relish (page 35) or Pork with Cider and Coriander (page 36).

COFFEE BAVARIAN CREAM

| 1.45* | 〇 | $ $ | 555 cals |

* plus 3 hours or overnight chilling

Serves 6

1 cup roasted coffee beans

3¾ cups milk

6 egg yolks

½ cup sugar

1 package unflavored gelatine

4 Tbsp water

1¼ cups heavy cream

2 Tbsp coffee-flavored liqueur

coffee dragees and coarsely grated chocolate, to decorate

1 To prepare (1 hour 30 minutes): Put the coffee beans in a saucepan and place over low heat for 2–3 minutes, shaking the pan frequently. Off the heat, pour all the milk into the pan, then return to the heat and bring to the boil. Remove from the heat, cover the pan and leave to infuse for at least 30 minutes.

2 Beat the egg yolks and sugar in a bowl until thick and light in color. The beaters should leave a ribbon trail on the surface of the mixture when lifted.

3 Strain on the milk and stir well. Pour into the rinsed out pan and stir over low heat for 10 minutes. Do *not* boil. Strain into a large bowl; cool for 20 minutes.

4 Sprinkle the gelatine over the water in a small heatproof bowl. Leave for 5 minutes until spongy, then stand the bowl in a pan of gently simmering water and heat until dissolved.

5 Stir the gelatine into the custard. Stand this in a roasting tin of cold water and ice cubes. Stir until the mixture is cool and about to set.

6 Lightly whip half of the cream to the thick pouring stage, then fold into the custard. Pour into a lightly oiled 5-cup moule-à-manqué cake tin or soufflé dish. Chill for at least 3 hours or overnight until completely set.

7 To serve (15 minutes): With dampened fingers, gently ease the edges of the cream away from the tin. Turn the cream out on to a flat plate, shaking the tin or dish gently until the cream moves and loosens inside the tin. Carefully ease off the tin and slide the cream into the center of the plate.

8 Whip the remaining cream until stiff, then gradually whisk in the coffee liqueur. Spoon into a piping bag fitted with a ½ inch star nozzle and pipe rosettes around the top edge of the cream. Decorate with coffee dragees and grated chocolate. Serve chilled.

Menu Suggestion

A classic dinner party dessert, Coffee Bavarian Cream would go well after a main course of Marinated Lamb Chops (page 30). Serve Nutty Camembert Pâté (page 13) to start.

BLACKBERRY ICE CREAM

| 0.40* | 🍴 | $ | ✳ | 436 cals |

* plus 1 hour cooling, 9 hours freezing and 2 hours softening

Serves 6

1 lb blackberries, fresh or frozen

2 Tbsp thick honey

⅓ cup sugar

14½ oz can evaporated milk, chilled

¾ cup heavy cream

2 Tbsp orange-flavored liqueur

3 Tbsp lemon juice

light cream and wafers, to serve

5 Remove from the freezer and beat well to break down the ice crystals. Return to the freezer for at least 6 hours.

6 *To serve* (5 minutes): Allow the ice cream to soften in the refrigerator for 2 hours. Scoop into individual glass dishes and serve with light cream and wafers.

Menu Suggestion
This is a sophisticated ice cream containing orange-flavored liqueur. Serve for a dinner party dessert after a light main course.

1 *To prepare* (35 minutes): Pick over fresh blackberries, wash and drain well. Place the berries in a small saucepan with the honey and sugar, cover the pan and cook gently for 5–10 minutes until soft.

2 Purée in a blender or food processor, then pass through a nylon sieve to remove seeds. Leave to cool for about 1 hour.

3 Whip the evaporated milk until it thickens slightly, then whisk the cream to the same consistency and fold gently together. Stir in the fruit purée with the liqueur and lemon juice.

4 Pour into a container (not metal). Freeze for about 3 hours or until set to a mushy consistency.

ICED ORANGE SABAYON

| 0.25* | 🍶 | $ $ | ✳ | 282 cals |

* plus 30 minutes cooling and 3–4 hours freezing

Serves 6

6 egg yolks

1 cup light brown sugar

6 Tbsp orange-flavored liqueur

1 cup unsweetened orange juice

glacé cherries and candied peel, to decorate

1 *To prepare* (20 minutes): Put the egg yolks and sugar in a bowl and beat together until pale and creamy. Stir in the liqueur and orange juice.

2 Pour into a medium-sized heavy-based saucepan. Stir over low heat until the mixture thickens and just coats the back of the spoon. Do *not* boil.

3 Pour into 6 individual soufflé dishes or ramekins and cool for at least 30 minutes. Freeze for 3–4 hours until firm. Wrap in plastic and return to the freezer.

4 *To serve* (5 minutes): Serve straight from the freezer, decorated with cherries and peel.

Menu Suggestion
Iced Orange Sabayon makes a good dessert to serve after a rich main course such as Creamed Seafood Vol-au-Vents (page 51).

Baking

Cakes and other baked desserts can be cooked ahead of time whenever you've time to spare, so that when the unexpected visitor calls there is always something delicious and homemade to offer. Why not plan a cook-ahead baking session one rainy day? Choose a few of the recipes in this chapter and plan to make them all at the same time. This makes economic use of oven space, saves on fuel bills and will stand you in good stead for future entertaining.

ORANGE MADEIRA CAKE

| 1.05* | $ | ✳ | 534 cals |

* plus 1 hour cooling and 1 day storing

Serves 6

12 Tbsp butter

1 cup sugar

3 eggs, beaten

1 cup self-rising flour

1 cup all-purpose flour

**finely grated rind of 1 orange and
    2 Tbsp juice**

1 cube sugar

1 To prepare (1 hour): Grease
and base line an 8½-inch spring-
form cake tin.

2 Put the butter or margarine
and sugar in a bowl and beat
together until light and fluffy.

3 Gradually beat in the eggs.
Sift the flours into the bowl,
then fold in with a large metal
spoon.

4 Fold in the grated orange rind
with the orange juice. Spoon
the mixture into the prepared tin.
Smooth the surface with a palette
knife.

5 In a strong plastic bag, crush
the cube sugar, then sprinkle it
evenly over the cake surface.

6 Bake in the oven at 325°F for
about 40 minutes until top is
golden, or until firm to the touch.
Cool 5 minutes in tin, then
unmold sides and cool on rack for
1 hour. Store for at least 1 day
before serving.

7 To serve (5 minutes): Cut
into 12 slices.

Menu Suggestion
This is a plain cake with a tangy
bite to it. Serve sliced at teatime,
or cut in thin wedges with Madeira
or port after dinner.

ORANGE MADEIRA CAKE
Madeira cake is well worth
making at home because it has a
much lighter texture and a more
buttery flavor than commercial
varieties. It is one of England's
most famous cakes, which gained
popularity in the 19th century,
when it was the tradition to offer
a slice of cake and a glass of
Madeira wine to morning callers.

BRAZIL FRUITCAKE

1.45* 🍰 $ $ ✳ 700–933 cals

* plus 1 hour cooling

Serves 6–8

12 Tbsp butter or margarine

1 cup sugar

3 eggs, beaten

1 cup Brazil nuts

$\frac{1}{2}$ cup candied lemon peel

1 cup dried apricots

1 cup light raisins

1 cup all-purpose flour

1 cup self-rising flour

2 tablespoons apricot jam, sieved and melted

8 oz marzipan and a few Brazil nuts, to decorate

1 To prepare (90 minutes): Line the bottom and sides of an 8-inch round cake tin or an 8-cup loaf tin with greased waxed paper.

2 Put the butter and sugar in a bowl and cream together until light and fluffy. Gradually beat in the eggs.

3 Chop or coarsely grate the nuts. Finely chop the candied peel. Snip the apricots into small pieces. Mix all the fruit and nuts together.

4 Sift the flours together and fold into the creamed mixture followed by the fruit mixture. Spoon into the prepared tin.

5 Bake the cake in the oven at 350°F for about 50 to 60 minutes. Cool for 10 minutes in the tin, then turn out on to a wire rack for 1 hour.

6 To serve (15 minutes): Brush the top of the cake with the apricot jam. Roll out the marzipan to fit the cake; press on top.

7 Crimp the edges and score the top in a diamond pattern. Decorate with the Brazil nuts. Grill the cake to brown the top. Store for up to 1 week.

Menu Suggestion
Serve Brazil Fruitcake instead of a traditional Christmas Fruitcake.

APPLE PARKIN

| 1.35* | $ | ✳ | 632–766 cals |

* plus 2 hours cooling and 2 days storing

Serves 6–8

| 1 lb eating apples |
| 2 Tbsp butter or margarine |
| 1½ cups all-purpose flour |
| 2 tsp baking powder |
| 3 tsp ground ginger |
| 4 Tbsp solid vegetable shortening |
| 1 cup rolled oats |
| ½ cup sugar |
| ½ cup light corn syrup |
| ½ cup molasses |
| 1 egg, beaten |
| 2 Tbsp milk |
| Cheddar cheese wedges, to serve |

1 To prepare (1½ hours): Grease and base line an 8 × 4-inch loaf tin. Grease bottom paper.

2 Peel, quarter, core and chop the apples. Melt the butter in a small saucepan, add the apples, cover and cook gently until soft. Beat the apples to a purée, then cool for about 30–40 minutes.

3 Sift the flour, baking powder and ginger into a large bowl. Rub in the shortening; stir in the oats and sugar.

4 Warm the syrup and molasses together until evenly mixed, then stir into the dry ingredients with the apple purée, egg and milk. Stir until evenly blended.

5 Turn into the prepared tin and bake in the oven at 350°F for about 1½ hours, covering loosely with foil after 45 minutes. Cool in pan 10 minutes.

6 Turn out of the tin and cool on a wire rack for 1 hour. Wrap and store for 2 days before eating.

7 To serve (5 minutes): Slice and accompany with wedges of Cheddar cheese.

Menu Suggestion

Yorkshire parkin is traditionally eaten with cheese, and the apples in this version go particularly well with it. Try it with a sharp Cheddar or Wensleydale for an unusual packed lunch.

FRUITY GINGERBREAD

| 1.05* | $ | ✳ | 175 cals |

* plus cooling and 3 days maturing

Makes about 16 squares

6 Tbsp butter or margarine
⅔ cup dark brown sugar
⅓ cup light corn syrup
⅓ cup molasses
1¾ cups rolled oats
1¼ cups self-rising cake flour
½ cup mixed dried fruit
2 tsp ground ginger
pinch of salt
¾ cup milk
butter for spreading (optional)

1 To prepare (1 hour): Melt the butter or margarine in a saucepan with the sugar, syrup and molasses.

2 Meanwhile, in a bowl, mix together the oats, flour, fruit, ginger and salt.

3 Pour the melted mixture into the bowl, then the milk. Beat vigorously with a wooden spoon until all the ingredients are evenly combined.

4 Pour the mixture into a greased and base-lined 9-inch square baking tin. Bake in the oven at 350°F for 50 minutes or until firm to the touch.

5 Allow to cool in the tin for 10 minutes, then turn out on to a wire rack and leave until cold. Wrap in plastic or foil and store in an airtight tin for 3 days until the gingerbread is really moist.

6 To serve (5 minutes): Unwrap and cut into about 16 squares. Spread with butter if desired.

Menu Suggestion
This moist gingerbread, with its added fruit, is bound to be popular with children. Pack a slice or two in the school packed lunch box.

ICED MARZIPAN ROUNDS

| 1.00* | 🍴 | $ $ | ✳* | 235 cals |

* plus 1 hour chilling, 30 minutes cooling and 30 minutes drying; freeze at the end of step 7

Makes 16

1½ cups flour
½ cup sugar
6 Tbsp butter or margarine
2 egg yolks
6 oz yellow-colored marzipan
2–3 Tbsp dark rum
¼ cup apricot jam
2 cups confectioners sugar
yellow food coloring

1 *To prepare* (1 hour): Mix the flour and sugar together in a bowl. Add the butter or margarine and rub in with the fingertips. Mix to a smooth dough with the egg yolks and 2 tsp water.

2 Turn the dough out on to a floured surface and knead lightly until smooth. Wrap and chill in the refrigerator for 30 minutes.

3 On a floured surface, roll the dough out to a ⅛ inch thickness. With a 2-inch round fluted cutter, stamp out 32 rounds. Prick with a fork.

4 Place the rounds on lightly greased baking sheets, then chill again in the refrigerator for 30 minutes.

5 Bake in the oven at 350°F for about 12–15 minutes. Transfer to a wire rack and leave to cool for 30 minutes.

6 Knead the marzipan with a few drops of the rum. Lightly dust the work surface with a little confectioners sugar, then roll the marzipan out to a ⅛ inch thickness. With the same 2-inch cutter, stamp out 16 rounds.

7 Brush each cooled cookie with a little melted apricot jam. Sandwich together with a marzipan round in the center.

8 Beat the confectioners sugar and remaining rum together. Divide in half. Add a few drops of coloring to one half.

9 Using small piping bags and plain nozzles, lattice the rounds with icing. Leave to dry for at least 30 minutes.

10 *To serve*: Serve immediately, or store in a single layer in airtight containers for up to 5 days.

Menu Suggestion
Make these unusual sandwich cookies for a special teatime treat. The children will love the marzipan and apricot jam filling, and the different colored icings make the cookies really eye-catching.

ICED MARZIPAN ROUNDS

Marzipan is another name for almond paste, made from sugar, almonds and egg white. The origins of marzipan are uncertain. Some say it was introduced to Europe by the Arabs, others that it was created by a French order of nuns. Literally translated, the word marzipan means "St Mark's bread," and European cuisines have a fair number of marzipan specialities connected with religious festivals. Sicily and Germany, for example, have marzipan fruits and vegetables at Christmas, whereas England has simnel cake at Easter and iced cakes with marzipan are served for Christmas and other celebrations.

LEMON AND LIME COOKIES

| 0.55* | $ | ✳* | 125 cals |

* plus 30 minutes cooling; freeze after cooling in step 4

Makes 24

$\frac{1}{2}$ **cup butter or margarine**
$\frac{1}{2}$ **cup sugar**
1 egg yolk
2 oz cream cheese
1$\frac{1}{4}$ cups all-purpose flour
finely grated rind of 1 small lemon
1 Tbsp lemon juice
4 tsp lime marmalade

1 *To prepare* (40 minutes): Put the butter or margarine and sugar in a bowl and beat together until light and fluffy.

2 Beat in the egg yolk, cheese, flour, lemon rind and juice, until a soft mixture is formed.

3 Place small spoonfuls of the mixture onto greased baking sheets, allowing room for spreading.

4 Bake in the oven at 375°F for about 15 minutes or until light brown. Transfer to a wire rack to cool for at least 30 minutes. Store in an airtight container for up to 3 days.

5 *To serve* (15 minutes): Melt the marmalade in a small saucepan and brush over the cookies, to glaze. Leave to set for 5 minutes before serving.

Menu Suggestion
With their tangy marmalade glaze, these cookies taste good at any time of day, but they go particularly well with morning coffee.

LEMON AND LIME COOKIES

These cookies are simplicity itself to make, almost like craggy, flat rock cakes. If you have a food processor, steps 1 and 2 can be made in moments, by working all the ingredients together in one go.

You will find the flavors of lemon and lime together are just perfect with a morning cup of coffee, but children may find the lime a little too tangy. You can of course use ordinary orange marmalade for the glaze if you wish, together with the finely grated rind of 1 small orange and 1 Tbsp orange juice, instead of the lemon in the recipe. This makes the cookies quite a bit sweeter.

ZIGZAG BATON

1.25*	🍴	$	1869 cals

* plus 24 hours rising, 1 hour at room
temperature and 1 hour proving

Makes one 1 lb loaf

$\frac{3}{4}$ cup milk and $\frac{1}{2}$ cup water, mixed
1 tsp sugar
1 package active dried yeast
1½ cups wholewheat flour
1½ cups bread flour
1½ tsp salt
2 Tbsp butter
beaten egg, to glaze
poppy seeds, to decorate

1 To prepare (35 minutes):
Warm the milk and water to
lukewarm. Pour half into a bowl
and stir in the sugar until
dissolved.

2 Sprinkle in the yeast, whisk
with a fork, then leave to stand
in a warm place for 10–15 minutes
until frothy.

3 Mix the flours and salt in a
warmed large bowl. Rub in the
butter with the fingertips.

4 Make a well in the center, add
the yeast and the remaining
milk and water and mix with a
wooden spoon. If too dry, add a
little more lukewarm water.

5 Turn the dough onto a floured
surface and knead for 10
minutes until smooth and elastic.
Place in a lightly oiled plastic bag
and leave to rise in the refrigerator
for 24 hours.

6 To serve (50 minutes): Remove
the risen dough from the
refrigerator and allow to come to
room temperature for 1 hour.
Turn on to a floured surface and
knead for 2–3 minutes to break
down any air bubbles.

7 Using both hands, roll the
dough into a sausage shape,
about 16 inches long. Place on a
greased baking sheet.

8 With a pair of sharp scissors
held at a 30° angle to the top
surface of the dough, make V-
shaped cuts about three-quarters
of the way through it at 2-inch
intervals.

9 Pull each section of dough out
to alternate sides to give a
"zigzag" appearance. Leave to rise
in a warm place for about 1 hour
or until doubled in bulk.

10 Brush the dough with
beaten egg, then sprinkle
with poppy seeds. Bake in the
oven at 450°F for 30 minutes until
golden. Cool on a wire rack before
serving.

Menu Suggestion
Serve this unusually shaped loaf
just as you would ordinary bread.
Made with half wholewheat and
half white flour, it has an
interesting texture and flavor.

Buffet Supper

A simple buffet supper is perfect for informal entertaining—say after the theater or a concert. This menu serves 8, but it can be easily adjusted for more or less. The Lamb and Mushroom au Gratin, a pasta dish like cannelloni, with a lamb, mushroom and tomato filling, can be made up to 1–2 days in advance, as can the Fresh Pineapple Compote. Simply pop the gratin dish in the oven and put the final decorations on the pineapple while your guests are having pre-supper drinks.

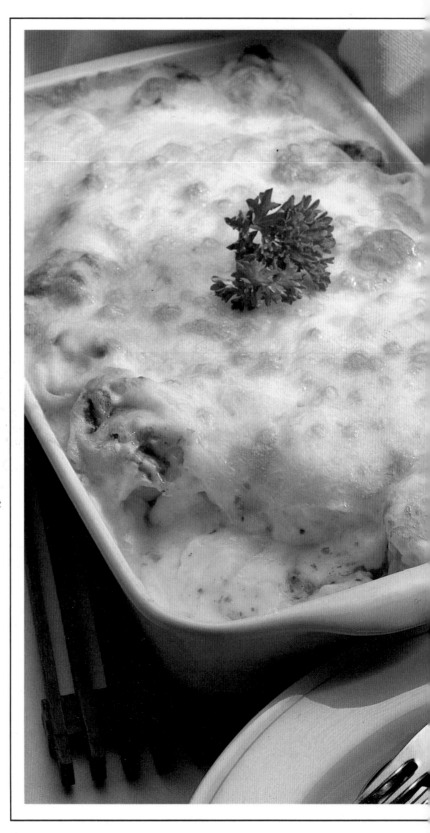

LAMB AND MUSHROOM AU GRATIN

2.00* | $ | ✳* | 566 cals

* plus 10 minutes cooling; freeze at the end of step 5

Serves 8

5 Tbsp butter
1½ lb mushrooms, finely chopped
1 Tbsp vegetable oil
1½ lb lean ground lamb
1 garlic clove, crushed
8 oz can tomatoes, drained
½ cup flour
1 Tbsp chopped fresh oregano or 1 tsp dried
1 Tbsp chopped fresh rosemary or 1 tsp dried
⅔ cup dry white wine
salt and freshly ground pepper
16 sheets cooked lasagne, about 10 oz raw weight
3¾ cups milk
4 oz Cheddar cheese, grated
4 oz Mozzarella cheese, grated or finely chopped

1 *To prepare* (1 hour 15 minutes): Melt 2 Tbsp of the butter in a large saucepan, add the mushrooms and cook over moderate heat for about 10 minutes until soft and reduced in volume.

2 Heat the oil in a large frying pan, add the lamb and brown well; drain off all the fat. Stir in the garlic, mushrooms, tomatoes, 2 Tbsp of the flour and the herbs. Cook for 1–2 minutes, then add the wine and seasoning to taste. Bring to the boil, then simmer for about 30 minutes, uncovered. Cool for 10 minutes.

3 Spread the mixture over the sheets of lasagne and roll up each sheet from one short side.

4 Cut the rolls into three. Pack tightly together, standing upright, in one large or two small 2-inch deep straight-sided ovenproof dishes.

5 Melt the remaining butter in a saucepan, add the remaining flour and cook over low heat, stirring with a wooden spoon, for 2 minutes. Gradually blend in the milk, stirring after each addition to prevent lumps forming. Bring to the boil slowly, then simmer for 2–3 minutes, stirring. Add plenty of seasoning, then pour over the pasta. Leave to cool, then cover and chill in the refrigerator until required.

6 *To serve* (45 minutes): Bake in the oven at 400°F for about 40 minutes. Uncover, sprinkle with the cheeses and broil until golden. Serve hot.

FRESH PINEAPPLE COMPOTE

| 0.50* | 🥘 | $ $ | 114 cals |

* plus overnight chilling

Serves 8

2 small ripe pineapples
4 Tbsp orange-flavored liqueur
1 lb 4 oz can lychees in syrup
shelled pistachio nuts, to decorate

1 *To prepare* (35 minutes): Cut each pineapple lengthwise into quarters, slicing through the crown at the top. Cut out the hard central cores and discard.

2 Using a serrated knife, carefully cut all around the edge of each pineapple boat between the flesh and the skin.

3 Carefully work the knife underneath the pineapple flesh, to release it completely from the skin. Cut the flesh into bite-sized cubes. Wrap the pineapple shells in plastic and set aside.

4 Put the pineapple cubes in a bowl and sprinkle over the liqueur. Drain the lychees, pouring the syrup into a saucepan. Add three-quarters of the lychees to the pineapple.

5 Boil the lychee syrup until reduced by half, then leave to cool. Add to the pineapple and lychees and fold gently to mix. Cover the bowl with plastic and chill overnight, with the pineapple shells and reserved lychees.

6 *To serve* (15 minutes): Cut the reserved lychees into flower shapes. Divide the pineapple and lychees equally among the 8 shells and pour over the syrup. Decorate with the lychee "flowers" and pistachios. Serve chilled.

FRESH PINEAPPLE COMPOTE

Canned lychees are available at most good supermarkets. They have a deliciously sweet flavor and unusual texture, and can be used in fruit salads of all kinds to add a touch of exotic interest. Lychees (also called lichees and litchis) are native to China, but they also grow in India and South Africa. The fresh fruit are available at some specialist markets and greengrocers in late summer, but they are not easy to recognize if you are only familiar with the canned fruit. The skin of fresh lychees is rough and brittle, almost like a bark.

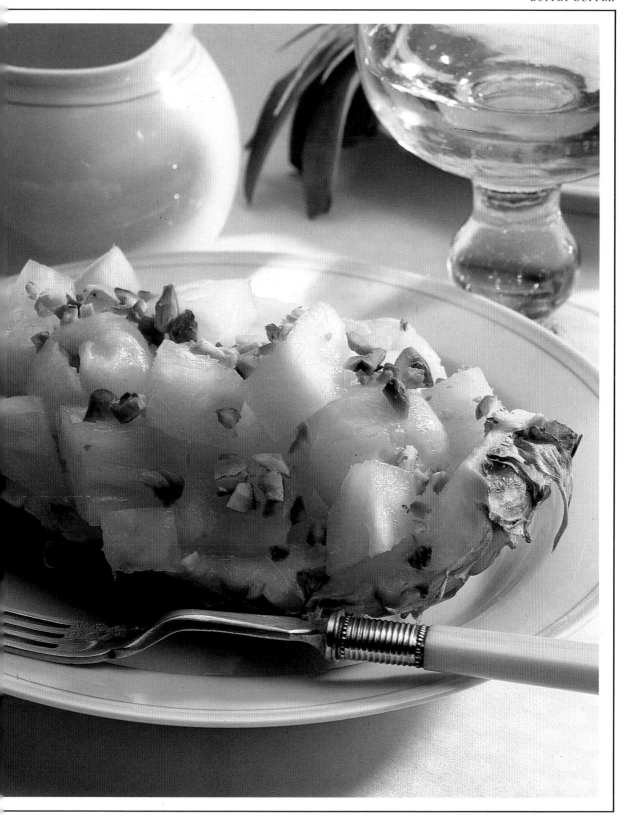

Cold Luncheon Party

For summer entertaining in the garden, nothing could be more relaxing than a cold luncheon party—especially when all the preparations can be done beforehand. Salmon in Puff Pastry makes a spectacular table centerpiece, and the two salad accompaniments complement each other perfectly. All you need to serve with them is plenty of crusty French bread and butter, and a selection of cheeses. Finish with the Open Pear Flan, and your guests will be amazed how perfect the food is, with no sign of cooking!

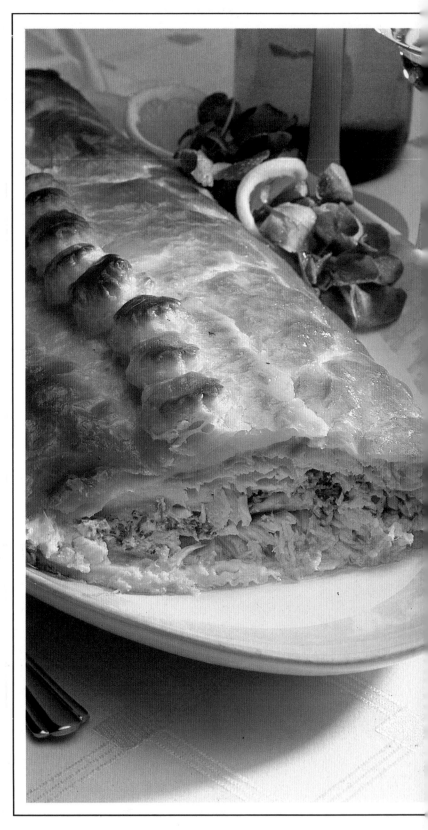

SALMON IN PUFF PASTRY

| 1.45* | $ $ | ✱* | 583–640 cals |

* plus 30 minutes chilling, 1 hour cooling and 30 minutes at room temperature

Serves 6

1 bunch watercress

3 Tbsp sour cream

finely grated rind of $\frac{1}{2}$ lemon

salt and freshly ground pepper

$2\frac{1}{2}$–3 lb salmon or sea trout, cleaned and filleted (see box)

1 quantity puff pastry (see page 157) or two 13 oz packages frozen puff pastry, thawed

beaten egg, to glaze

1 To prepare (1 hour 10 minutes): Wash the watercress and trim off the root ends. Chop roughly, then place in a bowl with the sour cream. Add the lemon rind and seasoning to taste, then stir until the ingredients are well mixed.

2 Using a sharp knife and holding the tail end of 1 salmon fillet, scrape the flesh away from the skin. Repeat with the other fillets.

3 Place two fillets skinned side down on a board and spoon on the prepared watercress filling. Top with the remaining fillets.

4 If using frozen pastry, stack one piece on top of the other. Roll out the home-made or frozen pastry to a rectangle about 12 × 9 inches.

5 Carefully place the fish on the pastry, leaving a $\frac{1}{4}$-inch border. Brush the edges of the pastry with beaten egg.

6 Fold the pastry over the fish to enclose it completely. Seal and trim. Lift on to a baking sheet and chill in the refrigerator for at least 30 minutes.

7 Use the remaining egg to glaze the pastry. Make 2 small holes in the pastry to allow the steam to escape. Place the baking sheet in the oven and bake at 400°F for about 45 minutes until the pastry is well risen and golden brown. To test, make a small slit through the thickest part of the fish—the flesh should begin to flake. Cool for at least 1 hour, then wrap in plastic or foil and refrigerate for up to one day.

8 To serve (35 minutes): Remove the salmon from the refrigerator and unwrap. Leave at room temperature for 30 minutes before serving.

SALMON IN PUFF PASTRY

Your fishmonger will clean the salmon for you, but to get four neat fillets, you may prefer to fillet it yourself. Cut off the head and tail and snip off the fins. Rinse the fish and pat dry. Place on a board, head end towards you, and snip along the belly from head to tail. Starting with the flesh nearest to the belly, ease the flesh away from the bones, using a filleting knife and short sharp strokes. Open out the fish and slide the knife tip under the end of the exposed bone. Using a similar action as before, work along the length of the fish to remove the bone completely. Pluck out any small bones in the flesh. Snip the skin between the halves to give two fillets, then neaten the edges. Repeat the process with the other fillet.

FENNEL WITH GREEN PEPPERCORN DRESSING

1.00* $ 103 cals

* plus 20 minutes cooling

Serves 6

3 heads of fennel

salt and freshly ground pepper

1–2 Tbsp lemon juice

$\frac{2}{3}$ cup heavy cream

1 Tbsp green peppercorns

2 tsp white wine or tarragon
    vinegar

1 To prepare (50 minutes): Trim any green leafy tops from the fennel and reserve. Cook the fennel in plenty of boiling salted water to which the lemon juice has been added, for 30–35 minutes or until just tender.

2 Drain well, then rinse immediately under cold running water. Cool completely; about 20 minutes. Cover and chill.

3 Lightly whip the cream. Roughly crush or chop the peppercorns, then fold them into the cream with the vinegar and seasoning to taste. Cover and chill.

4 To serve (10 minutes): Split the fennel heads in half and place on a flat serving dish. Spoon over the peppercorn dressing and garnish with the reserved snipped fennel tops.

PASTA AND ANCHOVY SALAD WITH GARLIC DRESSING

0.55*	406 cals

* plus at least 2 hours or overnight standing

Serves 6

two 2 oz cans anchovies in oil

3 Tbsp milk

12 oz small pasta shapes (see box)

salt and freshly ground pepper

1 garlic clove, roughly chopped

⅓ cup vegetable oil

juice of ½ lemon

6½ oz can pimientos, drained

4 Tbsp mayonnaise

1 To prepare (45 minutes): Drain the anchovies, place in a bowl and add the milk. Leave to soak for 30 minutes (this helps remove excess salt).

2 Meanwhile, cook the pasta in plenty of boiling salted water according to the packet instructions until *al dente* (tender but firm to the bite).

3 Drain the anchovies and rinse under cold running water. Pat dry with absorbent paper.

4 Reserve a few of the anchovies whole for garnishing and crush the remainder to a paste with the garlic. Add the oil and lemon juice gradually, whisking with a fork until thick. Add pepper to taste.

5 Drain the pasta and turn into a large bowl. Pour in the dressing immediately and toss well to mix. Leave to cool, then cover and chill in the refrigerator for at least 2 hours, or overnight if more convenient.

6 To serve (10 minutes): Cut the pimiento into thin strips. Add to the pasta salad, reserving a few for garnish. Add the mayonnaise and toss gently to mix. Taste and adjust seasoning. Pile the salad into a serving bowl and arrange the remaining whole anchovies and pimiento strips in a lattice pattern over the top. Serve at room temperature.

PASTA AND ANCHOVY SALAD WITH GARLIC DRESSING

Supermarkets and delicatessens now stock a huge variety of different pasta shapes, which make interesting salads as well as the more usual hot pasta dishes which are served with a sauce. For salads, don't buy the very tiny pasta shapes—these are only for use in soups. Choose small shapes such as *conchiglie* (sea-shells), which are excellent for trapping salad dressings and preventing ingredients sinking to the bottom of the salad bowl. *Fusilli* (spirals) and *farfalle* (bow ties) can also be used.

OPEN PEAR TART

| 1.20* | 🍳 | $ $ | ✳* | 464 cals |

* plus 1 hour cooling; freeze at the end of step 6

Serves 6

1½ quantities pâte sucrée (see page 158)

4 Tbsp butter

⅓ cup sugar

1 egg, beaten

½ cup ground almonds

4 tsp flour

2 tsp pear- or almond- flavored liqueur

3 ripe pears (Anjou or Bosc)

1 cup apricot jam

2 Tbsp water

1 To prepare (1 hour 10 minutes): Roll out the pâte sucrée on a lightly floured work surface and use to line a 10-inch loose-bottomed fluted tart ring. Prick the bottom with a fork and chill in the refrigerator for at least 15 minutes.

2 Meanwhile, put the butter and sugar in a bowl and beat together until light and fluffy. Beat in the egg and stir in the ground almonds, flour and liqueur. Pour into the pastry case and level the surface.

3 Carefully peel the pears, cut them in half lengthwise, and remove the core with a melon baller or teaspoon.

4 Lay each pear half cut side down, and cut them crosswise into thin slices. Keeping each pear half intact, place on the almond mixture to form the spokes of a wheel, then press each half slightly to fan out the pear slices.

5 Bake in the oven at 400°F for 10–15 minutes until the pastry just begins to brown. Turn the oven temperature down to 350°F and bake for a further 20–25 minutes.

6 Remove from the oven and cool for 1 hour. Store in an airtight container for not longer than 1 day.

7 To serve (10 minutes): Place the jam in a saucepan and add the water. Heat gently, stirring until the jam softens. Bring to the boil and simmer for 1 minute. Sieve and brush over the tart while still warm.

Midweek Party

Entertaining in the middle of the week can be a problem especially if you're out at work all day. With this simple three-course menu, everything can be prepared the night before, just leaving last-minute touches and soufflé-making before your guests arrive.

EGGPLANT AND CHEESE SOUFFLÉ

| 1.25 | 🍴 | $ | 454 cals |

Serves 4

1 lb eggplant

salt and freshly ground pepper

6 Tbsp butter

2 Tbsp flour

$\frac{2}{3}$ cup milk

4 oz Cheddar cheese, grated

4 eggs, separated

$\frac{1}{3}$ cup freshly grated Parmesan cheese

1 To prepare (45 minutes): Chop the eggplant roughly and place in a colander or sieve. Sprinkle liberally with salt and set aside to drain for 30 minutes. Rinse under cold running water, then pat dry with absorbent paper.

2 Melt 4 Tbsp of the butter in a saucepan, add the eggplant, cover and cook gently until golden brown and completely soft. Purée in a blender or food processor until nearly smooth.

3 Melt the remaining butter in a clean saucepan, add the flour and cook over low heat, stirring with a wooden spoon, for 2 minutes. Remove the pan from the heat and gradually blend in the milk, stirring after each addition to prevent lumps forming. Bring to the boil slowly, then simmer for 2–3 minutes, stirring.

4 Remove from the heat and stir in the eggplant purée, the Cheddar cheese, the egg yolks and seasoning to taste. Turn into a bowl, cover and chill in the refrigerator until required.

5 To serve (40 minutes): Lightly grease a 6-cup soufflé dish and dust out with all but $\frac{1}{4}$ cup of the Parmesan cheese.

6 Whisk the egg whites until stiff but not dry. Fold into the eggplant mixture until evenly combined. Spoon into the pre-pared dish and sprinkle with the remaining Parmesan. Bake in the oven at 400°F for 25–30 minutes. Serve immediately.

EGGPLANT AND CHEESE SOUFFLÉ

Making a soufflé is much easier than you think. Not only are soufflés quick, and therefore perfect for midweek entertaining, they are also ideal for making the night before and finishing off just before your guests arrive. Most savory soufflés have a simple base of thick béchamel sauce, to which chopped or puréed vegetables are added, often with a flavoring of cheese, as in this recipe. The secret of successful soufflé making lies at the end of the preparation. The egg whites must be stiffly whisked and then quickly folded into the thick sauce with a large metal spoon — to incorporate as much air as possible. Serve at once, before the soufflé starts to subside.

HUNGARIAN PORK

| 2.45* | $ $ | ✳* | 770 cals |

* plus overnight chilling; freeze at the end of step 7

Serves 4

1½ lb pork shoulder

1 medium onion, roughly chopped

1 large garlic clove, roughly chopped

2 oz stuffed green olives

¾ cup fresh white breadcrumbs

salt and freshly ground pepper

1 egg, beaten

2 Tbsp flour

1½ lb fresh spinach, trimmed and washed (see box)

¼ tsp grated nutmeg

4 Tbsp butter

1 lb ripe tomatoes, peeled and sliced

2 Tbsp vegetable oil

1 cup chicken stock

1 cup dry white wine

1½ tsp paprika

⅔ cup sour cream

extra paprika, to garnish

1 To prepare (1 hour 30 minutes): Trim the fat off the pork, then put through the grinder twice with the onion, garlic and olives. Turn into a bowl, add the breadcrumbs and seasoning to taste and mix well. Bind with the beaten egg.

2 With floured hands, roll the mixture into 36 small balls. Coat in the remaining flour, then chill for 30 minutes.

3 Meanwhile cook the spinach in a large saucepan with only the water that clings to the leaves. Drain well, then chop finely. Add the nutmeg and seasoning to taste.

4 Melt half the butter in a large frying pan, add the tomatoes and fry for 1–2 minutes. Transfer to an ovenproof casserole. Place the spinach on top.

5 Melt the remaining butter with the oil in the frying pan, add the meatballs in batches and fry over moderate heat until lightly colored on all sides. Remove from the pan with a slotted spoon and drain on absorbent paper.

6 Add the stock and wine to the frying pan and bring to the boil, stirring to scrape up the sediment from the base and sides of the pan. Add the paprika and seasoning to taste, then remove from the heat. Cool for 5 minutes, then stir in 3 Tbsp of the sour cream.

7 Put the meatballs on top of the spinach in the casserole, then pour over the sauce. Leave until cold, then cover and chill overnight.

8 To serve (1 hour 15 minutes): Cook in the oven at 400°F for 1¼ hours. Serve hot straight from the casserole or transfer to a serving dish. Drizzle with the remaining sour cream and the extra paprika.

HUNGARIAN PORK

It is not always possible to buy fresh spinach exactly when you want it, but frozen spinach can be used in this recipe with almost equal success. If you can, buy the frozen whole leaf spinach, as it tends to have more body than the chopped varieties. To make up the equivalent of 1½ lb fresh spinach for this recipe, you will need 12 oz–1 lb frozen. Thaw the spinach in step 3 by heating it gently in a heavy saucepan for about 10 minutes, stirring and breaking up any lumps with a spoon. If using leaf spinach, do not chop it or it will go too limp.

INDIVIDUAL PEACH MERINGUES

3.10* ✳* 319 cals

* plus cooling time; freeze meringue nests after cooling in step 4

Serves 4

2 egg whites

pinch of salt or cream of tartar

⅔ cup sugar

12 oz frozen raspberries

¾ cup confectioners sugar

4 Tbsp kirsch

2 ripe peaches

⅔ cup light cream

1 *To prepare* (2–2½ hours): Line a baking sheet with foil or non-stick baking parchment.

2 Put the egg whites in a bowl with the salt or cream of tartar. Whisk until very stiff. Add half of the sugar a little at a time, whisking after each addition until stiff peaks form. Fold in the remaining sugar lightly with a large metal spoon.

3 Fill a piping bag fitted with a large star nozzle and pipe the meringue into 4 "nests" on the lined baking sheet.

4 Dry out the meringues in the oven at 250°F for about 2 hours until they are firm and crisp. Transfer carefully from the baking sheet to a wire rack and leave until cold. Store in an air-tight tin for up to 1 week.

5 *To serve* (40 minutes): Put the raspberries in a bowl and sprinkle with the confectioners sugar and kirsch. Leave to macerate for about 30 minutes, folding gently to mix once the raspberries start to thaw.

6 Meanwhile, skin the peaches and halve and pit them. Cut the flesh into neat slices.

7 Spoon the raspberries into the meringue cases, then arrange the peach slices on top. Serve immediately, or the meringues will become soft. Hand the cream separately.

INDIVIDUAL PEACH MERINGUES

It isn't absolutely necessary to pipe these meringues, although it is very simple, and it does make them look extra special for a dinner party. If you haven't got a piping bag and nozzle, simply spoon 4 heaps of meringue on to the lined baking sheet and hollow out the centers with the back of the spoon, to make rough "nest" shapes. The meringue will hold its shape during baking exactly as it does when piped. If your meringues begin to brown too much during the baking time, simply prop open the oven door a little.

Portable Picnic

If you're planning a picnic, you want to be able to get up and go, especially if the weather promises to be good. All the recipes in this picnic menu keep and travel well, so you can make them and pack them ready the night before.

FRIED SALAMI CHICKEN

0.45*	593 cals

* plus 1 hour cooling time

Serves 6

12 chicken drumsticks, skinned

24 slices of salami (about 4 oz)

3 eggs, beaten

1 lb fresh breadcrumbs

vegetable oil for deep frying

3 Dip the salami-filled chicken first into beaten egg, then breadcrumbs and pat the crumbs in well. Repeat the egg and bread-crumb process to give a good coating.

4 Heat the oil in a deep-fat fryer to 350°F and fry the chicken for 7–10 minutes, until golden brown and cooked through. Drain on absorbent paper and leave to cool for about 1 hour.

5 *To serve* (5 minutes): Carefully remove the toothpicks from the drumsticks before packing.

1 *To prepare* (45 minutes): Make an incision to the bone along 1 side of each chicken drumstick and loosen the flesh around the bone.

2 Place 2 slices of salami around the bone, pull the chicken flesh together and secure with toothpicks.

FRIED SALAMI CHICKEN

Virtually any salami can be used for this recipe, but it is best to avoid fatty soft salami. Instead, choose a good Italian salami such as Genova or Napoli.

Hungarian salamis are also good, as is Cervelat, which is a partially dried sausage rather than a true salami.

ASPARAGUS AND BACON QUICHE

1.15* | 619 cals

* plus 1 hour cooling, and chilling

Serves 6

1½ lb fresh asparagus spears (about 24), or 8 oz frozen
1¼ cups flour
½ cup butter or margarine
about 4 Tbsp ice-cold water
4 oz thinly sliced bacon
4 eggs yolks
2 cups light cream
4 oz Gruyère cheese, grated
salt and freshly ground pepper

1 *To prepare* (1 hour 10 minutes): Trim the heads off fresh asparagus to the length of about 1½ inches. (Use the stalks for soup.) Blanch the heads in boiling salted water for 5 minutes; drain. If using frozen asparagus, cook in boiling water for 5 minutes, then drain and trim as above.

2 Put the flour in a bowl, add the butter and rub in with the fingertips until the mixture re-sembles fine breadcrumbs. Add enough ice-cold water to bind to a firm dough.

3 Turn the dough out on to a floured surface and roll out to fit a 10-inch fluted tart dish. Bake blind in the oven at 375°F for 15 minutes until set but not browned.

4 Meanwhile, with a knife, stretch the bacon on a flat surface. Wrap a small piece around each asparagus head.

5 In a bowl, mix the egg yolks with the cream, grated cheese and seasoning to taste. Spoon into the tart case.

6 Arrange the asparagus and bacon rolls in the custard. Reduce the oven temperature to 350°F and bake for 30–35 minutes or until set and golden brown. Cool for 1 hour, then wrap in plastic and store in the refrigerator until required (but not longer than 2 days).

7 *To serve* (5 minutes): Cut into wedges.

ASPARAGUS AND BACON QUICHE

To make a quick asparagus soup with the stalks not used in this recipe: chop the stalks and cook them in butter with a little finely chopped onion. Add 5 cups chicken stock, the finely grated rind and juice of ½ a lemon and salt and pepper to taste. Simmer for about 20 minutes until the asparagus is tender, then purée in a blender or food processor. Reheat with ⅔ cup light cream before serving.

SNOW PEA SALAD

| 0.20* | $ | 155 cals |

* plus 30 minutes cooling

Serves 6

8 oz snow peas, trimmed

salt and freshly ground pepper

2 Tbsp vegetable oil

1 cucumber

2 Tbsp light cream

3 Tbsp French dressing (see page 155)

chopped fresh parsley and mint

1 To prepare (15 minutes): Cook the snow peas in boiling salted water for about 4 minutes; drain and return to the pan. While still hot, add the oil and toss until well coated. Leave to cool for at least 30 minutes, then cover and chill in the refrigerator until required.

2 Cut the cucumber into 2-inch sticks, add to the snow peas, cover with plastic and chill in the refrigerator until required.

3 Whisk the cream and French dressing together with the parsley and mint, pour into a screw-topped jar and chill in the refrigerator until required.

4 To serve (5 minutes): Place the snow peas and cucumber in a salad bowl. Shake the dressing once more, pour over the vegetables and serve immediately.

POTTED CHEESE WITH MINT

0.20*	$	✳	409 cals

* plus at least 2 hours chilling

Serves 6

6 Tbsp butter, at room temperature

8 oz Cheddar cheese

1 Tbsp chopped fresh mint

4 Tbsp sour cream

freshly ground pepper

mint leaves, to garnish

brown bread or crispbreads, to serve

1 To prepare (15 minutes): Put the butter in a bowl and beat until really soft. Grate in the cheese, then beat it gradually into the butter.

2 Stir in the chopped mint and sour cream, adding freshly ground pepper to taste. (Salt should not be required as the cheese contains sufficient.)

3 Spoon into 4–6 individual serving dishes and garnish with mint leaves. Cover with plastic wrap and chill in the refrigerator for at least 2 hours.

4 To serve (5 minutes): Spread on slices of brown bread or crispbreads.

POTTED CHEESE WITH MINT

An English semi-hard cheese such as Red Leicester is excellent for making potted cheese because of its interesting orange-red color. It also has the right kind of flaky texture which blends smoothly and makes it easy to spread. Red Leicester is also a good melting cheese, so try it in cooking instead of Cheddar.

SPICED APPLE TORTE

| 1.20* | $ | ✳ | 627 cals |

* plus 1 hour cooling

Serves 6

| 12 Tbsp butter or margarine |
| 1 cup light brown sugar |
| $\frac{1}{2}$ cup bran |
| 1 tsp ground cinnamon |
| 1 lb cooking apples |
| finely grated rind of 1 lemon |
| 3 Tbsp lemon juice |
| 2 eggs, beaten |
| 1 cup self-rising flour |
| 1 tsp ground mixed spice |
| 1$\frac{1}{4}$ cups light cream, to serve |

1 *To prepare* (75 minutes): Melt 4 Tbsp of the butter or margarine in a saucepan. Add $\frac{1}{3}$ cup of the sugar and the bran and cinnamon and fry gently, stirring, until golden.

2 Spoon the mixture into a greased and lined 8-inch round cake tin.

3 Peel and core the apples, then slice them thinly into a bowl. Stir in the lemon rind and juice. Set aside.

4 Put the remaining butter or margarine in a separate bowl, add the remaining sugar and beat together until light and fluffy. Beat in the eggs gradually. Sift in the flour with the spice and stir in, followed by the apple mixture.

5 Spoon the mixture into the cake tin and level the surface. Bake in the oven at 350°F for about 50 minutes. Turn out on to a baking sheet lined with non-stick paper. Cool completely: about 1 hour. Cover and chill until required or for up to 2 days.

6 *To serve* (5 minutes): Unwrap, cut into wedges and serve with light cream.

SPICED APPLE TORTE

This cake tastes equally delicious with orange flavoring, so you can ring the changes each time you make it—which is bound to be often! Substitute the finely grated rind of 1 medium orange for the lemon rind, and the same quantity of freshly squeezed orange juice as specified for lemon in the recipe.

At the end of the summer when there are plenty of fresh pears about, you can use cooking pears such as Bosc, instead of the apples. Pears taste best with lemon, but you may prefer to use ground ginger rather than cinnamon, since ginger and pears have a special affinity for one another.

ENTERTAINING
FRIENDS
ON THE
WEEKEND

Saturday Lunch

Are friends or relations
arriving Saturday
lunchtime and staying
over until Sunday
afternoon? Make it a
relaxed weekend with
these suggested menus,
all of which can be
prepared in the days
leading up to the
Saturday, thus leaving
you free to enjoy the
company of your guests.
Start with an elegant
seafood and French bean
salad for Saturday lunch,
followed by homemade
bread rolls and cheese.
First impressions count!

SEAFOOD IN SAFFRON MAYONNAISE

| 0.55 | 🍴 | $ $ | 493 cals |

Serves 6

| 1 lb white fish fillets (haddock, cod or monkfish) |
| 1 bay leaf |
| 1 slice lemon |
| 4 oz peeled shrimp |
| 6 cooked, shelled mussels |
| few saffron threads |
| 1 egg yolk |
| ⅔ cup vegetable oil |
| 2 tsp white wine vinegar |
| salt and freshly ground pepper |
| 1 lb French beans, topped, tailed and cooked |
| chopped fresh parsley, to garnish |

1 *To prepare* (45 minutes): Place the fish in a large frying pan, cover with water and add the bay leaf and lemon slice. Bring to the boil, then immediately lower the heat and poach gently for 10–15 minutes until cooked. Strain off the poaching liquid, reserving 4 Tbsp. Cool the fish for at least 20 minutes.

2 Roughly flake the flesh. Place in a bowl with the shrimp and mussels, cover and chill for up to 2 days.

3 Meanwhile put the reserved fish liquor in a small saucepan, add the saffron threads and heat gently. Remove from the heat and leave to infuse until cold and golden yellow in color.

4 Put the egg yolk in a bowl and beat well. Beat in the oil a drop at a time, then continue adding in a thin, steady stream until the mixture is very thick. Stir in half the vinegar and continue beating in the oil until all is incorporated. Stir in the remaining vinegar.

5 Strain the saffron liquid into the mayonnaise and whisk to the consistency of light cream. Add seasoning to taste, cover and chill in the refrigerator for up to 2 days.

6 *To serve* (10 minutes): Arrange the French beans on a long serving dish. Pile the fish mixture down the center of the beans and spoon over the mayonnaise. Serve immediately, garnished with parsley.

SEAFOOD IN SAFFRON MAYONNAISE

Most good fishmongers sell monkfish, and if you can get it for this recipe, then you will find it better for a special occasion than cod or haddock. Although more expensive, its flavor is rather like that of lobster, and its flesh is very thick, firm and white—again like lobster, or scampi. Monkfish hasn't always been such a highly prized fish. Because of its unattractive appearance when whole, it used to be unpopular, but once the head is removed and the fish cut into fillets by the fishmonger, you need never know how ugly it was! In some areas it is known as angler fish or frog fish, and if you have eaten it in Mediterranean countries you will probably know it by either its Spanish name of *rape*, or by the French name *lotte* or *ange de mer*, or the Italian *rospo* (which means frog).

QUICK WHOLEWHEAT ROLLS

| 0.35* | $ | ✳ | 149 cals |

* plus 1 hour rising

Makes 12

2 tsp sugar

1¼ cups tepid water

1 package active dry yeast

1½ cups bread flour

1½ cups wholewheat flour

1½ tsp salt

1 Tbsp solid vegetable shortening

cracked wheat, to decorate

1 To prepare (35 minutes): Grease a baking sheet. Dissolve 1 tsp sugar in the water, sprinkle in the yeast and leave to froth for 15 minutes.

2 Sift the flours into a bowl with the salt and 1 tsp sugar. Rub in the shortening. Add the yeast mixture and mix to a soft dough. Turn on to a lightly floured surface and knead for about 2 minutes until smooth.

3 Divide the dough into 12 equal pieces and shape into rounds. Place on the greased baking sheet, brush with water and sprinkle the tops with cracked wheat. Cover with a clean damp tea cloth and leave to rise in a warm place for about 1 hour until doubled in size.

4 Bake at 450°F for 15–20 minutes or until golden brown. Cool for at least 15 minutes on a wire rack.

GARLIC AND BLACK PEPPERCORN CHEESE

| 0.45* | $ | ✳ | 113 cals |

* plus 2½–4 days draining and chilling
Makes 1 lb

2½ cups light cream
2¼ cups milk
2 Tbsp buttermilk
1 garlic clove
1 tsp salt
1 Tbsp chopped fresh mixed herbs
(parsley, chervil, chives, thyme)
2 Tbsp black peppercorns,
coarsely crushed
cucumber slices, to garnish

1 To prepare (35 minutes): Put the cream and milk in a saucepan and heat gently 90–100°F; stir in the buttermilk. Pour the mixture into a bowl.

2 Cover the bowl with plastic and leave in a warm place for 24–48 hours until the cream mixture turns to soft curds.

3 Line a colander with muslin or all-purpose kitchen cloth and place it in the sink. Pour the curds into the colander and drain for 10 minutes.

4 Place the colander on a rack in a saucepan, cover with plastic wrap and chill in the refrigerator for 18–24 hours.

5 On a board, crush the garlic to a smooth purée with the flat of a round-bladed knife and the salt. Spoon the curds from the colander into a bowl and stir in the mixed herbs, garlic and peppercorns.

6 Line a small plastic bowl or earthenware cheese mold with a double layer of damp cheesecloth or muslin, leaving a 2-inch overhang. Spoon in the curds and fold the cheesecloth over the top.

7 Invert the mold onto a wire rack placed over a shallow dish, cover tightly with plastic and chill for 18–24 hours.

8 To serve (10 minutes): Unmold the cheese onto a plate, remove the cheesecloth and garnish with cucumber slices. Serve chilled.

Saturday Dinner

This should be the high spot of the weekend. If you've planned not to eat out, then your menu at home should match that of the best restaurant in town! Start with a refreshingly tangy Avocado and Orange Salad with Citrus Dressing. Follow with a rich veal dish with wine, mushrooms and cream, which both looks and tastes very special, and yet is incredibly simple to prepare. Then finish the meal with Iced Strawberry Soufflé — a spectacular finale to any meal.

AVOCADO AND ORANGE SALAD WITH CITRUS DRESSING

0.40*	462 cals

* plus 1 hour or overnight chilling

Serves 6

$\frac{2}{3}$ cup vegetable oil

7 Tbsp freshly squeezed grapefruit juice

1 Tbsp snipped chives

$\frac{1}{2}$ tsp sugar

salt and freshly ground pepper

3 medium oranges

3 ripe avocados

1 *To prepare* (25 minutes): Put the oil in a screw-top jar with the grapefruit juice, chives, sugar and seasoning to taste. Shake well to mix.

2 Working in a spiral motion, remove the rind and white pith from the oranges with a serrated knife.

3 Cut the oranges into segments and place in a shallow dish. Shake the dressing again, then pour over the oranges. Cover the dish with plastic and chill in the refrigerator for at least 1 hour, or for up to 24 hours if more convenient.

4 *To serve* (15 minutes): Cut the avocados in half and twist to remove the pits. Peel off the skin, then slice the flesh neatly.

5 Remove the orange segments from the marinade and arrange on individual plates, alternating with avocado slices. Pour over the marinade and serve immediately.

VEAL ESCALOPES WITH CREAM AND MUSHROOM SAUCE

| 0.55* | 445 cals |

* plus cooling and chilling

Serves 6

6 veal escalopes, about 4 oz each

2 Tbsp flour

salt and freshly ground pepper

4 Tbsp butter

2 Tbsp olive oil

12 oz button mushrooms, sliced

1½ cups dry white wine

2 tsp chopped fresh tarragon or 1 tsp dried

1 cup heavy cream

tarragon sprigs, to garnish

1 To prepare (35 minutes): Trim each veal escalope to remove any gristle, then cut each one in half.

2 Place the escalopes well apart between sheets of non-stick paper or heavy-duty waxed paper. Pound well, using a meat mallet or rolling pin, until the escalopes are very thin. Remove paper, then coat the escalopes in the flour seasoned with salt and pepper.

3 Melt the butter with the oil in a heavy-based frying pan. Add the escalopes a few at a time and fry over moderate heat until lightly colored on both sides. Remove with a spatula and set aside on a plate.

4 Add the mushrooms to the pan and fry until the juices run. Add the wine and bring slowly to the boil, stirring, then return the escalopes to the pan, pile the mushrooms on top and sprinkle with the tarragon and seasoning to taste. Turn into a shallow dish. Leave to cool, then cover and refrigerate until ready to serve (overnight, if convenient).

5 To serve (20 minutes): Cook over moderate heat and bring slowly to the boil. Lower the heat, cover and simmer for 5–10 minutes until heated through. Remove the veal from the cooking liquid with a slotted spoon, arrange in a warmed serving dish and keep hot. Stir the cream into the pan and simmer until the sauce thickens. Taste and adjust seasoning, then pour over the veal. Serve immediately, garnished with sprigs of tarragon.

VEAL ESCALOPES WITH CREAM AND MUSHROOM SAUCE

Although veal is an expensive meat to buy, escalopes work out less so because they are beaten very thin and therefore weigh very little.

Escalopes come from the leg of the calf. The topside is the choicest cut, from which come the most tender escalopes. Slightly less expensive but still good are the escalopes from the loin. Some butchers sell escalopes cut from the "skirt" of the animal. These have a good flavor, but they do have a coarse grain which makes it necessary to cook them longer. Check with your butcher when buying so you can be sure of the cooking time.

ICED STRAWBERRY SOUFFLÉ

3.05* ⏣ $ $ ✳ 569 cals

* plus 1–2 hours setting, 3 hours
freezing, 2 hours softening

Serves 6

1 lb strawberries
4 Tbsp almond-flavored liqueur
2 Tbsp lemon juice
1 Tbsp confectioners sugar
1¼ cups heavy cream
3 Tbsp water
1 Tbsp unflavored gelatine
4 eggs, separated
1 cup sugar
1 pint strawberries
4–6 small ratafias or macaroons
⅔ cup heavy cream, whipped

1 *To prepare* (1 hour): Put half the strawberries in a bowl and stir in the liqueur, lemon juice and confectioners sugar. Cover and leave to marinate for 30 minutes.

2 Put the strawberries in a blender or food processor and work to a purée. Sieve to remove the seeds.

3 Tie a double band of waxed paper around the edge of a 5-cup soufflé dish to form a 2-inch collar. Stand a straight-sided 1 lb jam jar in the center.

4 Lightly whip the heavy cream until it just holds its shape.

5 Put the water into a small saucepan, sprinkle over the gelatine and leave to soak for about 5 minutes until spongy. Dissolve slowly over gentle heat.

6 Put the egg yolks and sugar in a bowl and whisk with an electric whisk until very light and creamy. Fold in the strawberry purée, whipped cream and dissolved gelatine.

7 Whisk the egg whites until stiff but not dry and fold into the strawberry mixture.

8 Pour the mixture into the prepared dish, keeping the jam jar in the center. Chill in the refrigerator for 1–2 hours until set, then transfer to the freezer for at least 3 hours, until firm.

9 *To serve* (2 hours 5 minutes): Remove the soufflé from the freezer and fill the jam jar with hot water. Twist gently to remove it. Fill the center with the remaining strawberries. Finely crush the ratafias or macaroons. Ease off the paper collar and coat the sides of the soufflé with crushed ratafias. Decorate with the whipped cream.

10 Transfer to the main body of the refrigerator for about 2 hours to soften before serving.

Sunday Brunch and Tea

Get off to a late, leisurely start on Sunday morning. Make a pot of fresh coffee to wake everyone up, then break open a bottle of Champagne—and treat your guests to the sumptuous sensation of fresh salmon. Before they leave, there's a special teatime treat—the fabulous French savarin, a ring of sweet yeast cake soaked in rum. Served with a medley of fresh fruits and cream, nothing could round off the weekend better.

FRESH SALMON KEDGEREE

| 0.45* | $ $ | 378 cals |

* plus cooling

Serves 6

12 oz fresh salmon

⅔ cup dry white wine

2 small onions, chopped

1 carrot, peeled and sliced

1 celery stalk, trimmed and chopped

1 Tbsp lemon juice

6 peppercorns

1 bouquet garni

salt and freshly ground pepper

1½ cups long-grain rice

4 Tbsp butter

1½ tsp English powdered mustard

3 hard-boiled eggs, shelled and quartered

cayenne pepper, to finish

celery leaves, to garnish

1 To prepare (10–15 minutes):
Put the salmon in a saucepan, pour in the wine and enough water to cover the fish. Add half of the chopped onions, the carrot, celery, lemon juice, peppercorns, bouquet garni and 1 tsp salt.

2 Bring slowly to the boil, then immediately remove from the heat. Cover the pan tightly with a lid and leave to cool. Chill in the refrigerator for up to 48 hours.

3 To serve (25–30 minutes):
Cook the rice in plenty of boiling salted water for 15–20 minutes until tender.

4 Meanwhile, remove the salmon from the liquid and flake the flesh, discarding skin and any bones. Strain the cooking liquid and reserve.

5 Melt half of the butter in a large frying pan, add the remaining onion and fry gently until soft. Drain the rice thoroughly, then add to the onion with the remaining butter. Toss gently to coat in the butter and stir in the powdered mustard.

6 Add the flaked salmon and the hard-boiled eggs and a few spoonfuls of the strained cooking liquid to moisten. Heat through. Shake the pan and toss the ingredients gently so that the salmon and eggs do not break up. Transfer to a warmed serving dish and sprinkle with cayenne to taste. Serve immediately, garnished with celery leaves.

FRESH SALMON KEDGEREE

Kedgeree, sometimes also called khichri, is a rice dish of Anglo-Indian origin. In the days of the Raj it was very popular for breakfast, made with smoked fish rather than the fresh salmon used here. Original recipes for kedgeree are made with curry powder or curry spices and the rice can be quite hot and spicy, but the delicate flavor of fresh salmon would be overpowered by pungent spices, so they are not used here.

Fresh salmon is a luxury, but for weekend guests it is well worth the expense. Look for salmon trout and farm trout, which are cheaper than the freshwater salmon.

FRUIT AND RUM SAVARIN

1.40* | $ $ ✳* | 568 cals

* plus rising, proving and cooling; freeze savarin only, at the end of step 7

Serves 6

1 package active dry yeast
3 Tbsp lukewarm milk
¾ cup bread flour, sifted with a pinch of salt
1½ cups sugar
2 eggs, beaten
4 Tbsp unsalted butter, softened
½ cup water
8 Tbsp dark rum
2 bananas, peeled and sliced
1 lb red grapes, halved and seeded
2 kiwi fruit, peeled and sliced
2 small oranges, peeled and segmented
light cream, to serve

1 *To prepare* (1 hour 30 minutes): Put the yeast in a warmed small bowl and add the milk; stir together. Add 3 Tbsp of the flour and beat well with a fork. Leave in a warm place for 10–15 minutes until frothy.

2 Put the remaining flour in a warmed large bowl with 1 Tbsp of the sugar and the eggs. Add the frothy yeast mixture, then beat until an elastic dough is formed. Cover with a floured tea towel; leave in a warm place until size doubles, about 30–40 minutes.

3 Beat the softened butter into the dough a little at a time until all is evenly incorporated.

4 Put the dough in a buttered and floured 1-quart savarin or ring mold. Cover with a floured tea towel and leave to prove in a warm place until it has risen to the top of the mold, about 35–40 minutes.

5 Uncover the mold and bake the savarin in the oven at 400°F for 25–30 minutes until risen and golden brown.

6 Meanwhile, make the rum sugar syrup. Put 1 cup sugar and the water in a heavy-based saucepan and heat gently until the sugar has dissolved. Bring to the boil and boil steadily, without stirring, for 5 minutes until syrupy. Remove from the heat and stir in 6 Tbsp of the rum.

7 Turn the savarin out onto a wire rack placed over a large plate or tray. Prick all over the savarin with a fine skewer, then slowly spoon over the warm syrup. Collect any syrup that drips on to the plate or tray and spoon it back over the savarin. Leave until completely cold. Transfer to an airtight tin until required (up to 48 hours).

8 *To serve* (10 minutes): Toss the prepared fruits together with the remaining 2 Tbsp sugar and rum. Place the savarin on a serving plate and pile the fruits in the center. Serve immediately with chilled light cream.

USEFUL INFORMATION
AND
BASIC RECIPES

Useful Hints

Planning your kitchen well and making full use of today's selection of labor-saving gadgets enables you to prepare and cook meals ahead of time, with a minimum of fuss.

KITCHEN PLANNING AND EQUIPMENT

Being successful with your last-minute preparations and keeping your cooking to a minimum may have a lot to do with how orderly and efficient your kitchen is and with the type of equipment you have. It goes without saying that kitchen equipment and utensils as well as electrical extras should be of good quality. Poorly designed or cheaply made items are never labor-saving.

THE KITCHEN
Nothing could be more an annoying than having a meal almost ready to serve and then having to waste time searching for a fish knife or a bottle of dried herbs. A simple rearrangement of storage areas could be a big step toward maximum efficiency. Divide your cupboards and drawers to avoid having to search for packages or utensils. Racks are available which

Racks on runners in drawers

are fixed or that pull out on runners. Make sure that everything you use regularly is within easy reach.

You should be able to move easily from sink to main work surface and then to the stove. Moving a sink is expensive but it may be possible to add a new work surface near it—either by fitting a large cutting board over the

draining surface or by placing a table near the sink. A cover fitted over the sink or a hinged work top

A cover over sink makes another surface

which is raised when needed are other ways to create extra work surfaces.

It may be a good idea to store regularly used condiments like mustard, vinegar, jam and sauces in a carousel on the table, thereby avoiding the need to get them out each meal time.

A kitchen with dining area opens up new possibilities for planning meals, as it allows the cook to stay with the diners throughout the meal. Especially good for informal entertaining, this arrangement allows you to prepare omelettes, chops and other quickly made dishes without interrupting the flow of conversation. A serving hole knocked through the dividing wall between kitchen and dining room is a good alternative. With these types of kitchens, good ventilation is very important to keep heat, steam and cooking smells to a minimum. A fan-activated hood over the cooker is the most effective method.

THE STOVE
Many new stoves come with automatic controls which enable you to set the oven to switch on at a pre-selected time and temperature. Food can be placed in the oven in the morning and be fully cooked when you come home in the evening. Most dishes can be placed in a cold oven and left without harm and brought up to

the correct temperature. Make sure that anything put in the oven for cooking later is thoroughly chilled. For example, a casserole should not be at all warm from the initial preparation of frying the meat and vegetables, otherwise dangerous bacteria may develop.

By making minor adjustments it is possible to cook several different dishes at the same time and temperature. To slow down the cooking of a pudding or poached fruit, simply cover the dishes with kitchen foil or stand the dish in a hot water bath. Roast meat using the slow method along with braised vegetables and roast potatoes.

POTS AND PANS

Choose casseroles which can withstand freezing and oven temperatures and which are attractive enough to use for serving and thus save on washing up. Make sure

Casserole dishes to suit all needs

they have tight-fitting lids, which is important with slow cooking to prevent moisture from escaping.

GADGETS

Sharp knives (and a steel or sharpener) are essential in the kitchen, but the cook who wishes to keep preparation work to a minimum will also need some of the specialized gadgets available. Which you buy depends on your needs, though most cooks would include a potato peeler and vegetable brush. *Apple corers* and

Specialized gadgets speed preparation

cherry pitters do their jobs very efficiently; *egg slicers* or *wedgers* are handy for making last-minute garnishes. A *garlic press* and *ice cream scoop* are extras you may also find worth acquiring. Wall can openers work faster and more easily than ordinary ones.

ELECTRICAL EQUIPMENT

It is all too easy to accumulate electrical appliances. Although they can help you to get through your work in the kitchen and are great time-savers, some may wind up gathering dust if you do not choose wisely. If there are not enough outlets in your kitchen to take all your appliances have your electrician install more.

The following items have features especially good for the busy cook who likes to prepare meals in advance.

FOOD PROCESSOR

With just the flick of a switch 1 lb meat can be ground in 20 seconds. A food processor greatly cuts down on preparation work. It does most of the jobs of a mixer and blender, though it does not whisk egg whites well. It chops, grinds, slices and grates as well as kneads bread. Many of the foods that you would normally need to prepare in advance can be done just before serving, therefore keeping them fresh. And if you do a lot of

quantity cooking for the freezer, or cook large quantities at one time, then a food processor will be a great help with large chopping and slicing tasks.

SLOW COOKER

A slow cooker enables you to prepare soups, stews or casseroles and then leave them for up to 12 hours to cook. In this way you can prepare a dish in the morning and come home to a fully cooked meal—the slow cooker is ideal for making all-in-one meals. There is no risk of burning or boiling dry. Some models have a removable pot which can be used for serving and makes cleaning much easier.

MICROWAVE OVEN

Food can be cooked in a microwave in about one-third the time it takes to cook it conventionally. Many foods take even less time—a baked potato will cook in 4 minutes, for example. A microwave oven is the perfect companion to food ready-prepared and frozen, as thawing can be done in the microwave and reheating takes only a few minutes. Flavor, texture and color remain unaltered when foods are reheated, and there is little risk of burning or sticking to the dish.

There are a number of different models available with varying degrees of sophistication—which one you choose largely depends on what extent you intend to rely on the microwave for cooking. Cooking is done by microwave energy for a set time. It is necessary to be present during cooking to turn food or to stir it because all microwave ovens have "hot spots" and do not cook food evenly. Turntables and stirrers help to reduce the amount of attention required. Cooking with a microwave oven is entirely different from conventional cooking. It is more precise and needs close attention for a short time. Some dishes may need to be finished off under the broiler if a browned appearance or crisp texture is wanted.

The Clever Cook

In this chapter you will find tips on how to cope with everyday cooking, as well as more special occasions, including Christmas. When time permits, preserves can be made for year-round use, and when you are in a hurry, the freezer can be used as a reliable standby.

PLANNING AHEAD

Although preparing and cooking meals can be a real pleasure, if it is your responsibility day after day it can easily become a chore. But with a little foresight and imagination you can find ways to do it when the mood strikes, or when you have spare time and are not rushed. In other words, cook ahead, and ensure that feeding your family always remains an enjoyable task.

PLANNING MEALS

There's a lot to be said for writing down your weekly menu plans. It helps you to think of ways to keep within the family budget and to make best use of your time. You can plan to cook extra meat on one

Serve leftover cold meat in sandwiches

night for serving later in the week or if you are having a family outing you could include pot-roasted meat for one meal and have leftover for serving cold in sandwiches. Plan different types of meals—not ones that all have to be started at the same time, or that all require last-minute attention.

Each meal should be nutrition-ally balanced and also include a variety of textures and colors as well as flavors. Avoid a sequence of rich sauces or too many pale-colored dishes. You wouldn't want to serve a creamy soup followed by a fish pie with a custard for dessert. On the other hand a creamy soup is an excellent choice if the main course consists of grilled lamb chops and some brightly colored vegetables. Make sure that the family is not begging for something crunchy to eat by the end of the meal. Offset a spicy meat dish with plain boiled rice or mashed potatoes.

SHOPPING

After noting what you have in store make out your shopping list. To save time always shop for several meals at a time. Most packaged foods are date stamped to tell you the minimum keeping time, after which flavor is impaired. Take advantage of fruit and vegetables when they are in season and combine low prices with best flavor.

Don't be too rigid about your list. An impulse buy may be a bargain, provided it doesn't mean having to juggle the entire meal plan. Also, you can't count on finding a certain ingredient, especially if it is fairly unusual. Have an alternative cut of meat or a different vegetable in mind in case what you originally planned turns out to be unavailable or exorbitantly priced.

COOKING A MEAL

To make life easier in the kitchen look at your chosen recipes and see how much can be made in advance. Does the recipe include a sauce (those without eggs or cream) which can be reheated without risk of curdling? Or you could make the stuffing before breakfast, or the dessert the night before?

Calculate the timing of each dish so that you can be sure you start cooking the one which takes longest first, and that all are ready together, or in the order required.

EASY ENTERTAINING

A successful dinner party starts with guests being greeted by a confident and calm host. Being organized is the key to success. Start by planning your menu well in advance and get as much as possible out of the way before guests arrive. Practical considerations like seating, table linen, flowers and fresh towels in the bathroom must be taken into account too. Buy your wine and any spirits well in advance, not forgetting garnishes like cocktail olives or onions.

A traditional three-course meal

For easy entertaining, stick to a traditional three-course meal. Any extras can consist of fruit and cheese *Never experiment*: always select dishes that you have made before. (To broaden your repertoire try out new dishes on your family first.)

Plan dishes which require only last-minute assembling, brief cooking or reheating. Start by choosing your main course, then pick a first and last course which balance it.

APPETIZERS

One certain way to make your entertaining easy is to avoid a hot first course altogether and serve something cold before guests assemble at the table. In this way you can easily slip off to the kitchen to do last-minute work on the main course. Crudités served with a spicy mayonnaise are always popular; also good for serving informally are stuffed mushrooms, a pâté or a mousse with toast.

Soups are also good first courses as they can be prepared in advance and simply reheated if they are to be served hot. Add any milk, yogurt or cream when reheating to avoid curdling.

MAIN COURSES

Select a casserole or stew which can be made in advance and served with vegetables which are cooked at the last minute. Conversely, serve broiled or fried foods, and have a vegetable casserole or ragout ready-prepared. If you plan to pan-fry escalopes or steaks, then make sure you have enough frying pans to cope with all the frying at the

Equipment for deep-fat frying

same time. For deep-fat frying have everything ready beforehand, together with any last-minute garnishes.

DESSERTS

Most cold desserts can easily be made in advance. Gelatine-based desserts like cheesecakes and cold mousses only become firm after at least 4 hours in the refrigerator.

Serve light simple desserts after a substantial main course and rich luxurious ones after a light meal.

MEAT AND POULTRY

Meat and poultry, especially chicken, continue to be a favorite choice for many family meals. It's important for the busy cook to find a good friendly butcher and stick to him. If he appreciates your business he will be more likely to do some of the more fiddly and time-consuming tasks such as boning a shoulder of lamb and chopping or grinding meat to the size you require for a particular dish.

Plan to buy enough meat to allow for leftovers which can be made into another main course. You may wish to buy enough meat at one time for the whole week and do most of your meat cooking on the weekend when you have time. Allow 4–5 oz boneless meat per serving and 5–12 oz meat on the bone per serving (depending on how much bone).

Bear in mind that the larger a piece of meat the longer it will keep: for example, ground meat should be used on the day of purchase, whereas a large roast will keep for up to 5 days in the coldest part of the refrigerator. If you do buy your meat all at once you may wish to cut it yourself, and for this you must have a good sharp kitchen knife. The food processor is a great time saver for grinding meat, but remember that ground meat should not be

Keep meat wrapped loosely in foil

prepared more than 12 hours in advance or blood will ooze out and the meat become dry. Wrap meat loosely with foil to allow air to circulate, otherwise it will deteriorate rapidly. (Never leave meat in sealed plastic bags.)

Poultry should be used within 24 hours of purchase; frozen birds *must* be completely thawed before cooking. When preparing a bird for roasting, never place warm stuffing in a cold bird unless you are about to put it straight into a hot oven, otherwise dangerous bacteria may develop. Prepare stuffing in advance, but refrigerate it separately until just before roasting.

Although chops and steaks are always popular and take very little time to cook, they are expensive. To add variety to meals, choose from the more economical cuts and cook stews and casseroles.

STEWS, CASSEROLES AND BRAISED DISHES

Almost all stews and casseroles improve in flavor if made at least

Removing solid fat from stew

24 hours ahead. Allow them to cool, then cover and refrigerate. The fat will rise to the surface and become solid, making it easy to degrease the dish—especially important for oxtail and other fatty meats. They will keep covered in the refrigerator for up to 3 days.

Beef is the favorite meat for this long, slow and moist form of cooking, which tenderizes the tougher cuts. Most cuts of pork and lamb are tender and so long

slow cooking is not so often used, but some cuts can make excellent casseroles. Boiling fowls are very good value, but tough and require slow cooking. When cooking stews and casseroles on the stove they must be very slowly simmered—if allowed to boil the meat will toughen. Stir occasionally to prevent sticking and check to see if more liquid is needed. Cooking these dishes in a casserole in the oven is easier, as no attention should be required provided that the temperature is sufficiently low, but unless other items can be cooked at the same time it is less economical. Single

Moistening braised meat with stock

large pieces of beef are excellent braised in the oven on a bed of chopped vegetables moistened with stock.

If you plan to reheat a stew or casserole, undercook vegetables, particularly root vegetables which will crumble if overcooked, either by cutting in larger-than-usual pieces, or adding halfway through. Add green vegetables and any chopped fresh herbs when reheating. Enrich fricassees and blanquettes with egg and/or cream when reheating to avoid curdling. Reheat in a 350°F oven. Sliced meats are best reheated with a little gravy added to keep them moist.

MARINADES

A marinade is a great way to prepare meats in advance. Flavored with herbs and spices, a marinade will add flavor to meat and also help tenderize it.

Marinades also help prevent meat from spoiling and in some cases it may be left to marinate for several days. Immerse the meat in the

Immersing meat in a marinade

marinade, cover and refrigerate until ready for cooking. With poultry, flavor will penetrate better if it is skinned first.

FISH

Fish requires very little cooking time, making it a good choice for midweek family meals when you are on a tight schedule and have little time to spend in the kitchen. But it can be a fiddly task to prepare fish for cooking, so patronize a fishmonger who will clean and fillet fish for you. Otherwise, you can prepare fish up to 12 hours before cooking, but make sure you use a good sharp knife. Keep the fish in the refrigerator, loosely wrapped to prevent the flesh from drying out. The fish can then be broiled or fried. *Avoid overcooking*—most fish needs as little as 5 minutes on each side.

Allow 6–8 oz of fish per serving, depending on whether it is a fillet or whole fish. Fresh fish should be cooked on the same day; smoked fish can be kept for 2–3 days in the refrigerator.

Fish needs to be kept moist as it easily dries out. Fish casseroles can be made in advance and reheated just before serving, but make sure that the fish is submerged in liquid. With white fish like cod and haddock, cook extra and use the leftovers for fish pies, fish cakes or croquettes, or to serve cold in a salad. To pre-cook fish for pies etc, cover with cold water and bring to the boil. Turn off the heat and leave for 5 minutes, then drain. With frozen fish, leave for 10–15 minutes. Do not be tempted to leave any longer as it will become soggy. The cooking liquid can be set aside as the basis for a sauce. Leave the fish to cool, then fork into flakes, removing the skin and bones.

Marinating is a good way to keep fish moist during storage.

Ceviche, a Mexican dish using raw fish, makes an excellent

Turning fish chunks in a marinade

dinner-party starter. Use firm white fish chunks and marinate in lemon juice for up to 12 hours, though 1 hour is all that is needed; turn the fish once during marinating. Salmon marinated in lime juice is also delicious. Toss the fish with chopped sweet peppers in a garlicky vinaigrette.

Once shellfish are removed from their shells they very quickly dry out. This is especially so with molluscs like mussels, oysters and scallops. Avoid preparing these in advance unless you wish to incorporate them in a cold fish salad or in a soup or sauce. Have ready pancakes or vol-au-vent cases to make a lunch dish which needs only last-minute assembling and reheating.

Remember that canned fish is a useful standby. Use canned tuna or salmon for mixing with rice or pasta for a quick midweek meal, or for making a party mousse.

COOK-AHEAD FISH DISHES

FISH CAKES

Makes 10

1 lb mealy potatoes (peeled weight), cooked
12 oz leftover cooked cod or haddock fillet, flaked
2 Tbsp butter or margarine
4 Tbsp chopped fresh parsley
finely grated rind of $\frac{1}{2}$ lemon
salt and freshly ground pepper
flour
2 eggs, beaten
1$\frac{1}{2}$ cups fresh breadcrumbs
vegetable oil, for shallow frying

1 Mash the potatoes and stir in the fish, butter, parsley, lemon rind and seasoning to taste.

2 When the mixture is cool but not cold, turn out on to a lightly floured surface.

3 With floured hands, shape into a sausage about 15 inches long. Make sure that the surface is free from cracks.

4 Cut the roll into ten 1$\frac{1}{2}$-inch slices. One at a time, place the slices on a floured surface and pat with a palette knife to level the surface and reduce the thickness to about $\frac{3}{4}$ inch.

5 Coat the fish cakes one at a time in the beaten eggs, then in the breadcrumbs. Chill in the refrigerator for at least 30 minutes or until required.

6 When ready to serve, put enough oil in a frying pan to come about halfway up the fish cakes. Heat until a cube of bread turns golden brown in 50–60 seconds. Lower in a few cakes and fry until golden brown. Turn over and cook for a further 5–10 minutes.

7 Drain well on absorbent paper while frying the remainder.

FREEZING INSTRUCTIONS
Prepare the fish cakes to the end of step 5. Open freeze on baking sheets until firm. Pack into rigid containers and return to freezer. Thaw for 2 hours only and complete as in steps 6 and 7.

FISH CROQUETTES

Makes 12

4 Tbsp butter or margarine
¾ cup flour
1¼ cups milk
12 oz leftover, cooked white fish, flaked
2 Tbsp finely chopped parsley
1 Tbsp capers, roughly chopped
1 tsp lemon juice
salt and freshly ground pepper
cayenne pepper
1 egg, beaten
¾ cup dried breadcrumbs
vegetable oil, for deep-frying

1 Melt the butter in a saucepan, add half the flour and cook over low heat, stirring with a wooden spoon, for 2 minutes.

2 Remove the pan from the heat and gradually blend in the milk, stirring after each addition to prevent lumps forming. Bring to the boil slowly, then simmer for 2–3 minutes, stirring. Cover and leave for at least 30 minutes until cold.

3 Stir the fish into the sauce, beating until smooth. Stir in the parsley, capers and lemon juice, mixing well. Season with salt, pepper and cayenne.

4 Turn the mixture onto a board, divide in half, then into 12 fingers. With *lightly* floured hands, roll each portion into a sausage about 3 inches long.

6 When ready to serve, heat the oil in a deep-fryer to 350°F. Place a few croquettes at a time into a frying basket and lower gently into the hot oil. Deep-fry for 2–3 minutes or until golden brown. Drain on absorbent paper while deep-frying the remainder.

FREEZING INSTRUCTIONS

Prepare the croquettes to the end of step 5. Open freeze on baking

sheets until firm. Pack into a rigid container and return to the freezer. Thaw for 2 hours only; complete as in step 6.

MARINADE FOR RAW FISH

Serves 4

1 tsp coriander seeds
1 dried red chili, seeded and roughly chopped
juice of 4 limes
juice of 2 lemons
2 Tbsp olive oil
freshly ground black pepper
1 medium onion, finely sliced
1 lb fish fillets (monkfish, flounder, sole)

1 Crush the coriander seeds and chili to a fine powder in a mortar. Mix with the lime juice, lemon juice, olive oil, pepper and onion rings. (Do not add salt as this draws the juices out of the fish making the dish very watery.)

2 Pour over the fish, mix well, cover and chill in the refrigerator for at least 6 hours or until the fish turns opaque or white.

FRUIT

A bowl of fruit saves many busy cooks from the time and trouble of making a dessert. The various textures, colors and flavors of fruit make it a good choice to finish off any meal, especially a substantial one where the refreshing taste of fruit is welcome.

Choose fruit which is slightly underripe for serving several days after buying. Store underripe fruit at room temperature; to speed up

Ripen fruit in a brown paper bag

ripening, place the fruit in a brown paper bag and tie tightly. Store ripe fruit in the refrigerator. Pick over and wipe soft berry fruits, discarding any damaged ones. Other fruits can be washed in advance and given a good polish with absorbent paper. Grapes, however, should be washed just before serving to keep their bloom.

Gluts and other fruit bargains usually mean that the fruit is ripe and must be used very soon. Make sure that you have the time to prepare the fruit either for the freezer or for making preserves. Adding sugar to fruit will help keep it for longer in the refrigerator. Make fruit purées and freeze for 6–8 months, or store in the refrigerator for 2–3 days; use to make fools and fruit mousses or serve as a sauce for ice cream.

If you are after a trouble-free impressive dessert select exotic (though expensive) fruits such as mangoes, kiwi fruits and papayas

to add to a fruit salad. When serving cut-up fruit remember that bananas, apples and peaches should be left until the last moment and sprinkled with lemon juice to prevent discoloration. Lemon juice also heightens the flavor of a fruit salad. Keep cut fruit in the refrigerator, tightly wrapped with plastic.

Fruit puddings like crumbles and fruit pies can be made up to the baking stage in advance, or pre-baked, then warmed through just before serving. Meringue shells and pie cases can be made several days ahead of time and filled with fruit, cream or ice cream just before serving.

CHEESE

Whether you serve cheese on its own or with fruit, it makes an interesting and satisfying conclusion to a meal. Always keep cheeses well covered before serving, otherwise they will dry out around the edges very quickly. Wrap them individually to prevent flavors from mingling. They are best stored in an airtight container in the larder; if kept in the bottom of the refrigerator take out 30 minutes before serving. Soft cheeses will keep for up to 10 days and hard cheeses for up to 1 month.

Fresh cheeses like *fromage blanc* and *petits suisses* are ideal for serving with soft berry fruits. Cheddar and other hard cheeses are good companions to apples and pears as well as nuts. Soft cheeses like Brie and Camembert go well with grapes.

VEGETABLES

Vegetables are a vital part of most meals because they add valuable nutrients and fiber and help to balance them. But it is important that they be prepared and cooked properly. It is all too easy to sacrifice vegetable texture, nutrition and flavor in the name of expediency.

Most vegetables can be prepared up to 12 hours before serving (but remember that there will be a nutrient loss); after that flavor is slightly impaired. They should be tightly covered with plastic and stored in the refrigerator until ready for cooking. Root vegetables such as potatoes and turnips should be kept in cold water in the coldest part of the refrigerator. (However, vitamin C, which is water soluble, starts to diminish.) Celeriac, Jerusalem artichokes and salsify need to be soaked in water with lemon juice or vinegar added to prevent discoloration.

Many vegetables need only to be cooked briefly before serving. Some, like carrots, green beans or cabbage, are best when they are still crisp and almost crunchy and in this way more nutrients are retained. They can be slightly undercooked, then rinsed under

Rinsing vegetables to arrest cooking

cold running water to retain color and arrest further cooking. Reheat quickly in butter just before serving.

Vegetable dishes can be cooked in a number of different

ways to help keep last-minute preparations to a minimum.

Braised Vegetables like red cabbage, celery, endive and celeriac are delicious when braised, that is, slowly cooked in very little liquid until they become soft. Leave until cold, cover and refrigerate, then reheat slowly.

Stewed Ratatouille (vegetable ragout) is the classic example of a dish which improves greatly if made well ahead of serving (see recipe on page 22). Stewed vegetable dishes will keep for 2–3 days in the refrigerator. They are also good served cold (allow them to come to room temperature for best flavor).

Stuffed Serve vegetables as an accompaniment stuffed with breadcrumbs, or as a main course stuffed with rice and chopped meat. The stuffing can be made in advance and the case filled up to 12 hours ahead. Bake in the oven to finish. Choose from tomatoes, eggplants, mushrooms and onions.

Puréed Most vegetables can be puréed, either as a convenient way of storing them in the freezer for later use in soups, or as a vegetable dish accompaniment. Boiled or steamed vegetables can be quickly puréed in a blender or food processor or put through a sieve or vegetable mill. Leave until cold, cover and refrigerate. To reheat, season, add a dash of cream and heat slowly, stirring often. Root vegetables can be put in the oven.

COOK-AHEAD VEGETABLE DISHES

LAYERED FRENCH-STYLE POTATOES

Serves 4–6

2 lb potatoes, peeled
2 Tbsp Dijon mustard
2 Tbsp snipped chives
1¼ cups milk or chicken stock
salt and freshly ground pepper
2 Tbsp butter, melted

1 Cut the potatoes into ½-inch slices and arrange one layer in a greased 5-cup ovenproof dish.

2 Combine the mustard, chives, liquid and seasoning. Pour some over the potato layer. Repeat layers of potato and mustard/chive dressing, finishing with potato.

3 Brush the top layer of potato with butter, and sprinkle with salt and pepper. Cover the dish with foil and leave in a cool place until required.

4 When ready to serve, bake in the oven at 350°F for 1¾–2 hours until the potatoes are tender when pierced with a fork.

STUFFED PEPPERS

Serves 4

3 Tbsp butter
1 onion, chopped
4 oz bacon, chopped
4 tomatoes, peeled and sliced
1 cup long-grain rice, cooked
4 Tbsp grated Cheddar cheese
salt and freshly ground pepper
4 large green peppers
¾ cup fresh breadcrumbs
⅔ cup chicken stock

1 Melt 2 Tbsp of the butter in a heavy-based saucepan, add the onion and bacon and fry gently until golden brown. Add the tomatoes, cooked rice, half of the cheese and seasoning to taste.

2 Halve the green peppers lengthwise; remove pith and seeds. Place them in a single layer in a greased ovenproof dish and spoon in the stuffing.

3 Mix the remaining cheese with the breadcrumbs and sprinkle over the stuffing. Pour the stock around the peppers and top each with a pat of butter. Leave in a cold place until required.

4 When ready to serve, bake in the oven at 375°F for 15–20 minutes, or until the peppers are tender.

RICE AND PASTA

Rice and pasta are essential store-cupboard items to add variety to meals. They can be served in place of potatoes as an accompaniment to meat or poultry, or as a main course in their own right. They are both an excellent way to stretch leftover meat and vegetables.

RICE
Rice takes very well to a number of seasonings and flavorings so that family members need never tire of it. Cook extra rice to use cold in a rice salad or as part of a stuffing for vegetables or meat. Allow $\frac{1}{4}$ cup raw rice per serving.

Fluffing up rice before serving

Plain boiled rice can be made up to 24 hours ahead of serving. To reheat, dot with butter or margarine and place in a 350°F oven for 20 minutes. Fluff up with a fork and serve. Risottos, paellas and pilafs can be reheated in the same way.

PASTA
Along with dried pasta, a good supply of fresh pasta, now so readily available, is a good reserve in the freezer. It takes only 1–2 minutes to cook from frozen and with a good pasta sauce on hand you can quickly serve a delicious no-fuss dinner party dish. Cook extra pasta shapes to add to soups and salads (pasta to be served cold should not be tossed in butter which hardens it).

Many pasta sauces can be made in advance and gently reheated. Delicious dishes can also be made in minutes by tossing pasta in such basics as cheese, eggs and cream and topping with grated Parmesan cheese. Fresh herbs, canned fish or crisp bacon are good last-minute additions.

Cooked pasta is best stored coated in a sauce, and in made-up dishes such as macaroni cheese and lasagne (which also freeze well). It will keep for several days in the refrigerator and can be reheated in a 350°F oven for 20 minutes or so until bubbling.

COOK-AHEAD SAUCES TO SERVE WITH PASTA

MILANESE SAUCE
Serves 4

2 Tbsp butter
$\frac{1}{2}$ onion, chopped
2 oz mushrooms, chopped
8 oz tomatoes, peeled and chopped, or 15 oz can tomatoes, drained
1 tsp sugar
1 bay leaf
few sprigs of thyme
pinch of grated nutmeg
salt and freshly ground pepper
2 oz ham, chopped
2 oz tongue, chopped

1 Melt the butter in a heavy-based saucepan, add the onion and mushrooms and fry gently for 3–5 minutes until soft. Stir in the tomatoes, sugar, herbs, nutmeg and seasoning to taste. Cover and simmer gently for about 20 minutes, until the sauce has thickened and developed a good flavor.

2 Add the ham and tongue and simmer, uncovered, for a further 5–10 minutes. Cool, then chill in the refrigerator or freeze until required. Reheat for 5–10 minutes until bubbling, then taste and adjust seasoning before serving.

BOLOGNESE SAUCE
Serves 4

1 Tbsp butter
2 oz bacon, chopped
1 small onion, chopped
1 carrot, peeled and chopped
1 celery stalk, washed, trimmed and chopped
8 oz lean ground beef
4 oz chicken livers, chopped
1 level Tbsp tomato paste
$\frac{3}{4}$ cup dry white wine
$1\frac{1}{4}$ cups beef stock
salt and freshly ground pepper

1 Melt the butter in a large saucepan, add the bacon and fry for 2–3 minutes. Add the onion, carrot and celery and fry for a further 5 minutes until just browned.

2 Add the beef and brown lightly, then stir in the chicken livers and cook for a further 3 minutes. Add the tomato paste and wine and simmer for a few minutes more.

3 Stir in the stock and seasoning to taste and simmer for 30–40 minutes, until the meat is tender. Cool, then chill in the refrigerator or freeze until required. Reheat for 5–10 minutes until bubbling, then taste and adjust seasoning before serving.

PORTABLE FOOD

Whether it's for a simple packed lunch or an elegant picnic, food must be the kind that can be prepared ahead of serving, and it must travel well. Food must remain fresh and appetizing during storage, which may not always be in ideal conditions. Sandwiches are always a good choice, but there are many other possibilities for adding variety to portable foods.

Choose foods that are firm but moist, and that will not become limp in transport. Filled things like sausage rolls, deviled eggs and meat turnovers which can be eaten with the fingers are good, as are cold cooked chicken portions, and omelettes, cooked, cooled and sliced. Hard-boiled eggs, pizzas and quiches also add interest to picnics.

Remember too that a can of sardines or tuna fish, a jar of olives and some homemade pickles are good cupboard items for last-minute outings. Buy good fresh bread and some cheeses and you have satisfying picnic fare.

A carefully planned picnic does not have everything made ahead. Some dishes are best assembled at the site and in fact make picnics more enjoyable. Include plenty of fresh salad ingredients and fresh fruits, plus several sharp knives and a small cutting board for slicing. Take along a good home-made vinaigrette. Cold vegetables like marinated mushrooms and ratatouille can be made in advance and travel well.

Plastic drinking mugs and paper plates make picnics easy. If you regularly enjoy picnics it may be worth having a hamper. It not only adds style to a picnic but it saves searching for bottle and can openers and assembling plates and cups as everything is ready for transport. Vacuum bottles, especially ones with wide-neck openings, open up possibilities of taking along hot foods such as soups or a warming chili con carne or beef stew.

If you take a flask of tea or coffee, carry the milk separately in a special plastic container, or an unopened carton; it ruins the taste if added in advance.

DEVILED CHICKEN DRUMSTICKS

Makes 6

$\frac{2}{3}$ cup vegetable oil
1 tsp mild curry powder
1 tsp paprika
$\frac{1}{2}$ tsp ground allspice
$\frac{1}{2}$ tsp ground ginger
6 chicken drumsticks

1 Make the marinade. Whisk together the oil and spices.

2 Skin the chicken drumsticks. Using a sharp knife, make 3 shallow slashes in the flesh of each one.

3 Spoon the marinade over the chicken, cover and chill in the refrigerator for 4–5 hours, turning occasionally.

4 Place the chicken drumsticks in a roasting tin just large enough to hold them in a single layer. Pour over the marinade.

5 Bake in the oven at 400°F for 40–45 minutes, basting frequently and turning once. Cool on a wire rack.

6 When completely cool, wrap a little foil over the end of each drumstick, or top with a cutlet frill. Pack together in a rigid container for transporting.

SANDWICHES

A good sandwich starts with good bread; don't overlook wholewheat, rye or pumpernickel breads which can go a long way in adding variety to sandwiches. Fresh bread is hard to slice thinly enough for sandwiches, so use a day-old loaf, or buy it ready sliced.

Using an electric carving knife

Alternatively, use an electric carving knife, which will happily cut newly baked bread into wafer-thin slices. Pita bread makes a good pocket for filling with a variety of salads and cold meats. Warm the bread in the oven and wrap tightly in foil. Do not grill the bread or it will become brittle when cold.

Make sure butter for spreading is at room temperature; or use tub margarine. Both provide a good waterproof protection for the bread, preventing it from becoming soggy, and stick the sandwich together. Spread it right to the edges.

Choose fillings with contrasting textures and cover the bread completely—there is no skimping with a good sandwich. Tuck in lettuce and tomatoes at the last-minute to prevent sogginess. Mayonnaise is a good addition.

Sandwiches can be made in advance and stored overnight. Wrap them individually in plastic and store in the refrigerator.

BEEF PATTIES

Makes 10

1 medium onion, chopped
1 lb lean ground beef
1 beef bouillon cube, crumbled
1 Tbsp chopped fresh oregano or
   1 tsp dried
1 egg, beaten
salt and freshly ground pepper
3 Tbsp vegetable oil
1½ cups flour
½ tsp salt
6 Tbsp shortening
4 Tbsp butter or margarine
beaten egg, to glaze

1 Mix together the onion, ground beef, crumbled stock cube, oregano and egg. Season lightly.

2 With wet hands, shape the mixture into 10 flattened balls.

3 Heat the oil in a large frying pan and cook the patties for 4–6 minutes on each side. Drain and cool on absorbent paper.

4 Put the flour and salt in a bowl, add the shortening and butter or margarine and rub in with the fingertips. Mix to a soft dough with about 2½ Tbsp cold water.

5 Turn the dough on to a floured surface and knead lightly until smooth. Roll out thinly, then stamp out 10 rounds with a 2½-inch fluted cutter and 10 rounds with a 4-inch fluted cutter.

6 Place the cool patties on the smaller circles of dough, brush the edges with beaten egg and cover with the larger circles. Seal the edges well.

7 Cut the pastry trimmings into tiny rounds. Brush the patties with beaten egg, decorate with the rounds and brush with more beaten egg.

8 Place the patties on a baking sheet and bake in the oven at 375°F for 20–25 minutes until golden. Cool on a wire rack for 30 minutes before packing in a rigid container.

CARROT AND PINEAPPLE SLAW

Serves 4

4 tsp vegetable oil
4 tsp vinegar
4 tsp pineapple juice from can
pinch of sugar
dash of mild curry paste
4 rings canned pineapple
1 lb carrots, scraped
4 Tbsp light raisins
salt and freshly ground pepper

1 Put the oil in a rigid container with the vinegar, pineapple juice, sugar and curry paste. Cover and shake well to mix.

2 Using scissors, snip the pineapple into the dressing. Grate in the carrot, using the coarse side of the grater. Stir in the raisins and seasoning to taste.

3 Seal the container and chill in the refrigerator until required.

SPINACH AND APPLE SALAD

Serves 8

1 lb fresh spinach
4 Tbsp orange juice
2 Tbsp vegetable oil
1 Tbsp wine vinegar
salt and freshly ground pepper
2 large eating apples

1 Pull off any thick stalks from the spinach. Wash the spinach, drain well and shred. Chill in a large plastic container.

2 Mix the orange juice, oil, vinegar and seasoning together. Quarter, core and slice the apples and stir into the dressing. Pour into a covered container, cover and chill.

3 Toss the spinach and dressing together just before serving.

CHRISTMAS COUNTDOWN

To ensure that you have a festive but calm Christmas, start shopping and planning for your holiday entertaining well in advance. There's no substitute for a complete holiday checklist covering Christmas lunch and all the traditional Christmas goodies plus table decorations. It may seem daunting at first, but with foresight and organization Christmas time can be the pleasure it is supposed to be.

The best way to plan a Christmas period of eating without frustration in the kitchen is to keep meals, other than Christmas lunch, flexible. A roast ham or ham along with leftover turkey will provide several meals if you plan a good selection of winter salads to serve with them. Have some cold desserts such as a fruit compote or brandied peaches on hand or make a Christmas cheesecake with a cranberry topping, or a chestnut pavlova—meringue layers can be made several days before assembling and stored in an airtight container.

A freezer will be of enormous help when preparing for Christmas. All baking can be done about 3 months in advance. Freeze pies and breads uncooked and bake them nearer the time of serving . . . part of the enjoyment of Christmas is the delicious smells wafting from the kitchen. Make your own mincemeat; providing brandy is added it can be made at the beginning of December or even earlier. Plum puddings are traditionally made at the end of November.

- Buy a bird large enough to serve your guests with leftovers. Calculate the size of bird you need on the basis of 12 oz–1 lb for small birds, 12 oz for medium birds, 8 oz for large birds per serving. Order it early.

- Make sure you allow shelf space in the freezer for Christmas food. Mark packages for Christmas.

- If you make your own preserves and pickles, pot some in small attractive jars and set aside for entertaining over Christmas; they also make excellent last-minute gifts.

- Make your sauces in advance and have a few on hand to enliven leftovers. Keep all sauces in the refrigerator.

Sauce	In advance
Brandy Butter	2 weeks
Cumberland Sauce	1 week
Cranberry Sauce	1 week
Bread Sauce	2 days
Horseradish Sauce	1 day (using fresh cream)
Vinaigrette	1 week

- Make a large quantity of white sauce and store in $\frac{1}{2}$ pint portions. It will keep for up to 5 days in the refrigerator. Add cheese or herbs to it when reheating and serve with vegetables or use as the basis for a turkey casserole.

- Peel potatoes up to 24 hours in advance. Soak in cold water and keep in the coldest part of the refrigerator.

- Peel chestnuts and cook the day before serving. Leave to cool and store tightly wrapped in the refrigerator along with ready-trimmed Brussels sprouts.

- Check drinks cupboard and take advantage of Christmas specials frequently offered. *Buy or order early.* There are usually special offers for buying wine by the case. Remember to stock up on ice cubes. Turn them into plastic bags; to keep cubes separate spray them with soda water.

CHRISTMAS PLUM PUDDING

Makes 1 pudding to serve 8

1 cup prunes
$1\frac{1}{2}$ cups currants
$1\frac{1}{2}$ cups seedless raisins
$1\frac{1}{2}$ cups light raisins
$\frac{3}{4}$ cup flour
$\frac{1}{4}$ tsp grated nutmeg
$\frac{1}{4}$ tsp ground cinnamon
$\frac{1}{2}$ tsp salt
$\frac{3}{4}$ cup fresh breadcrumbs
$\frac{1}{2}$ cup shredded suet
$\frac{2}{3}$ cup dark brown sugar
$\frac{1}{4}$ cup chopped blanched almonds
finely grated rind of $\frac{1}{2}$ lemon
$\frac{2}{3}$ cup stout ale
2 eggs, beaten

1 Snip the prunes into small pieces into a large bowl, discarding any pits.

2 Half-fill a steamer or large saucepan with water and put it on to boil. Grease a 6-cup pudding basin or bowl.

3 Add the remaining ingredients to the prunes and stir well until evenly mixed.

4 Spoon the mixture into the prepared bowl, pushing down well. Cover with greased, pleated waxed paper and foil. Steam for about 8 hours.

5 Remove the foil covering, but leave the paper in position. Allow to cool, then cover with a clean dry cloth or foil and store in a cool place for at least 2 weeks before serving.

6 To reheat, steam for $2\frac{1}{2}$ hours. Turn out onto a warmed serving plate and serve with brandy or rum butter.

MINCEMEAT

Makes about $5\frac{1}{2}$ lb

1 lb currants
1 lb light raisins
1 lb seedless raisins
2 cups chopped mixed peel
2 cups hard cooking apples, peeled, cored and grated
1 cup chopped blanched almonds
1 lb dark brown sugar
12 Tbsp shredded suet
1 tsp grated nutmeg
1 tsp ground cinnamon
finely grated rind and juice of 1 lemon
finely grated rind and juice of 1 orange
$1\frac{1}{4}$ cups brandy

1 Place the dried fruits, peel, apples and almonds in a large bowl. Add all the remaining, ingredients and mix thoroughly.

2 Cover the mincemeat and leave to stand for 2 days. Stir well and put into jars. Cover. Leave for at least 2 weeks to mature before using.

FESTIVE CHRISTMAS CAKE

8-inch round fruit cake
apricot glaze (see page 144)
$1\frac{1}{4}$ lb marzipan or almond paste
2 lb royal icing (see page 144)
ribbon and Christmas cake decorations such as Santa Claus, snowmen, robins, reindeer or Christmas trees, to finish

1 At least 14–20 days before required, place the cake on a 9-inch cake board. Brush with apricot glaze and cover with marzipan (see page 144). Loosely cover the cake and store in a cool dry place for 4–5 days.

2 Using half the royal icing, roughly spread the icing over the top and side of the cake. Leave to dry for 24 hours. Keep the remaining icing in a covered container.

3 Spoon the remaining icing on top and roughly smooth it over with a palette knife.

4 Using a palette knife or the back of a teaspoon, pull the icing into well-formed peaks.

5 Using a palette knife, smooth a path down the center of the top and side of the cake. Leave to dry for about 24 hours.

6 Place a piece of ribbon along the pathway, securing the ends with pins. Arrange the decorations on top, securing them if necessary with little dabs of freshly made icing. Leave to dry for at least another 24 hours, ideally about 1 week before Christmas.

7 Once iced, the cake will keep fresh without an airtight tin, but when dry, protect it by covering with a cake dome or box.

TO COVER A CAKE WITH MARZIPAN

Cover the cake with marzipan 1 week or—at the latest—2 days before applying the first coat of royal icing. If the marzipan is not given enough time to dry out, oil from the paste may discolor the icing.

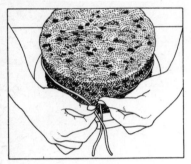

1 To cover a round or square cake, first measure round the cake with a piece of string.

2 Dust your work surface liberally with confectioners sugar and roll out two thirds of the marzipan to a rectangle, half the length of the string and twice the depth of the cake.

3 Trim the edges of the marzipan neatly with a knife, then cut the rectangle in half lengthwise.

4 Place the cake upside down on a board and brush the sides with apricot glaze. Gently lift the marzipan and place it firmly in position round the cake. Smooth seams with a palette knife and roll a jam jar lightly round the cake.

5 For a square cake, position one strip of marzipan on one side of the cake and fold it round to cover a second side. Repeat for the other two sides. Keep the top edge of the cake square with the marzipan.

6 Smooth the seams with a palette knife and mold any surplus marzipan into the bottom edge.

7 Brush the top of the cake with apricot glaze. Dust your working surface with confectioners sugar and roll out the remaining marzipan to a round or square the same size as the top of the cake.

8 Lift the marzipan onto the top of the cake with the rolling pin. Lightly roll with the rolling pin, then smooth the seam and leave to dry for at least 2 days.

APRICOT GLAZE

Makes 1 cup

| 1 cup apricot jam |
| 2 Tbsp water |

Put the jam and water in a saucepan and heat gently, stirring, until the jam softens. Bring to the boil and simmer for 1 minute. Sieve the glaze and use while still warm.

ROYAL ICING

Makes about 2 lb

| 4 egg whites |
| 2 lb confectioners sugar |
| 1 Tbsp lemon juice |
| 2 tsp glycerine |

1 Whisk the egg whites in a bowl until slightly frothy. Then sift and stir in about a quarter of the confectioners sugar with a wooden spoon. Continue adding more sugar gradually, beating well after each addition, until about three quarters of the sugar has been added.

2 Beat in the lemon juice and continue beating for about 10 minutes until the icing is smooth.

3 Beat in the remaining sugar until the required consistency is achieved, depending on how the icing will be used.

4 Finally, stir in the glycerine to prevent the icing from hardening. Cover and keep for 24 hours to allow air bubbles to rise to the surface.

PRESERVES

Putting food by is an age-old tradition which ensures that seasonal fruits and vegetables do not get wasted and are available all year round. Making jams, jellies and marmalade, or spicy pickles, relishes and chutneys is still one of a cook's most rewarding tasks, as the results should be not only less expensive but better than anything in the shops.

Special equipment is not essential for making preserves, but some help to make the job easier. Preserving pans are thick-based with slanting sides which help prevent overboiling of a hot mixture. Choose a good one made from heavy aluminium or stainless steel; it can double as a pan for making pickles and chutneys which contain a lot of vinegar. Brass, copper and iron react with vinegar causing a metallic flavor, so pans of these metals must not be used when making pickles and chutneys. A nylon sieve should be used as metal can discolor fruit and it also reacts adversely with vinegar. A long-handled wooden spoon makes stirring easier and if you make jellies, then a jelly bag is worth having. Other useful aids for regular jam-makers are a sugar thermometer and a jam funnel.

Jars must be in perfect condition with no cracks or chips. Use only jars made expressly for canning, and always use new lids for a proper seal. Sterilizing the jars before use is essential—make sure they are thoroughly clean by washing in hot soapy water and rinsing well. Use while warm so that they do not crack when filled with boiling jam or chutney.

JAMS, JELLIES AND MARMALADES

Which preserve you make is largely a matter of family preference, but there are several points that the busy cook needs to consider. When a favorite fruit is abundant, it may not be a convenient time for you to make preserves. If you have a freezer, then most fruits can be frozen for use later (raspberries, for example, have a short season) otherwise only buy a large amount if you know you will have the time to preserve them immediately.

Jams, jellies and maramalades all require patience and time— time to clean and trim fruits, time to cook, and time to process. Use only top-quality fruit and be careful dealing with hot liquids.

FRUIT

There must be sufficient quantities of pectin, acid and sugar present in fruit for preserves to get their characteristic firm set. Getting the balance right is what successful preserve making is all about, so it is important to follow recipes exactly until you get the knack of creating your own combinations of fruits. Fruit which is just ripe or only slightly underripe should be used; pectin content diminishes in overripe fruit. Fruits low in acid or pectin can still be used, but they require the addition of a fruit high in pectin, commercial pectin, and/or acid. Lemon juice helps to bring out the flavor of the fruit but commercially bottled pectin may be used according to manufacturer's instructions. Allow 2 Tbsp lemon juice for every 4 lb fruit.

Equipment needed for making preserves

SUGAR

Once the fruit has softened, sugar is added; sugar not only affects setting quality, it also acts as a preservative. If too little sugar is used, then the preserve may not set properly. Too much sugar and the preserve may crystallize and become sticky. To ensure that the preserve sets well, the sugar must be added after the fruit has sufficiently softened—which is why uncooked fruit for preserving should not be frozen in a sugar pack.

First dissolve the sugar slowly in the hot fruit, then boil briskly until setting point is reached. To help retain the natural color and flavor of the fruit, it is important that you do not greatly exceed the stated time for boiling in the recipe testing.

TESTING FOR A SET

A sugar thermometer can be placed in, or stood in or attached to, the

Using a sugar thermometer

side of the pan. When the temperature reaches 220°F, a set should be obtained. Or use the saucer test: place a little spoonful of the preserve on a chilled saucer, leave to cool, then push your finger gently through it. If the surface wrinkles, setting point has been reached. The pan should be removed from the heat during this

Using finger to test for a set

test. If setting point has not been reached, then return to the boil for a few more minutes and test again. Once setting point has been reached, remove any scum from the surface with a skimmer or slotted spoon before potting.

JELLIES

To make a clear, firmly set jelly, strain the fruit and add the sugar to the extracted juice. Fruit is cooked to a pulp and left to drip through a jelly bag (though you

Straining fruit pulp through jelly bag

can improvise by using a double thickness of fine cloth, the four corners tied to an upturned chair) until all the juice is strained off. Fruit high in pectin can be re-cooked after the first straining in a little water and then strained again. Measure the juice and for every $2\frac{1}{2}$ cups juice, add 1 lb sugar to fruit juices high in pectin and 2 cups sugar for juice with a medium pectin content. The fruit juice and sugar are then boiled until setting point is reached.

MARMALADE

To prepare citrus fruits, the juice is squeezed out and the peel is cut thinly or thickly according to how you like your marmalade. The seeds and pith, which are rich in pectin, are loosely tied in a piece of muslin and cooked along with the citrus juice, peel and water. A large amount of water is used with marmalade because of the long cooking, during which it should reduce by about half. After

Squeezing muslin bag to extract liquid

cooking, squeeze the muslin bag with a wooden spoon to extract as much liquid as possible. An alternative method is to cook the fruit whole: after simmering the fruit is cut and the seeds and pith boiled for a few minutes before adding the sugar.

When cooking frozen oranges, use the whole-fruit cooking method and add one-eighth extra weight of fruit to offset pectin loss during freezing.

CANNING, SEALING AND STORING

Jars holding around $\frac{1}{2}$ pint or 1 pint are the usual choices. The jars should be warm and placed on a heat-resistant surface such as a chopping board or a pile of news-papers to prevent cracking when ladling in the hot preserve. Fill the jars up to the bottom of the neck. Some wholefruit jams and marmalades should cool for about 15 minutes before potting, other-wise the fruit will rise. Some people still cover jellies with parafin, but most recommendations nowadays are to process jellies, jams, and preserves in a hot water bath. If using only a parafin seal, limit it to jellies (no jams or preserves) that have a very firm set. Then immediately cover with a lid. Label with contents and date.

Store in a cool, dry, dark place for up to 1 year. If stored for longer, the flavor and color will start to deteriorate although the preserve is perfectly safe to eat. If mold growth occurs on the top of a jam, it is not safe to eat.

PICKLES, CHUTNEYS AND RELISHES

All of these are a good way to add interest to any meal, be it hot or cold, elaborate or plain.

Many kinds of fruit and vegetables are used, ranging from onions, red cabbage, cucumbers, cauliflower, apples and dried fruit to eggplants, bananas and pears.

Pickles are preserved either raw or lightly cooked. They should look attractive, so produce must be perfect. For most types no more than washing and trimming is needed. Chutneys and relishes need more preparation as ingredients must be finely chopped. Chutneys are cooked long and

Spices add extra flavor to vinegar

slowly to produce a jam-like consistency. Relishes are cooked briefly or not at all.

All are preserved in vinegar, which must have an acidic content of at least 5%. Distilled (white) vinegar is best for light-colored pickles; cider vinegar is traditional for pickled onions and perfectly good for chutneys. The more expensive wine vinegars give the best flavor.

Spices add the finishing touch. They are usually ground for chutneys and relishes, left whole for pickles.

MAKING PICKLES
Before vinegar is added, many vegetables and some fruits are first salted to remove excess water, which would dilute the strength of the vinegar during storage, and therefore diminish the keeping qualities. Vegetables with a high

Layer with salt before adding vinegar

water content like squash, tomatoes and cucumbers are layered with salt. Use 1 Tbsp salt for every 1 lb vegetables. Other vegetables like cauliflower and onions are covered with a brine solution of $\frac{1}{3}$ cup salt dissolved in $2\frac{1}{2}$ cups water for every 1 lb vegetables. The vegetables are left, covered, for up to 24 hours, then drained and rinsed. Fruits do not require brining as they are usually lightly cooked to evaporate the surplus moisture before pickling.

Pouring vinegar on pickles

Pack vegetables loosely and attractively in warmed jars. Pour over cold vinegar for crisp pickles and hot vinegar for softer ones. Fill jars leaving only a small space for expansion during processing and making sure that the vinegar covers the contents. Cover immediately with canning lids and process as directed by jar manufacturer.

For sweet fruit pickles, sugar is added to the vinegar, the liquid is reduced to concentrate the flavor and poured over the fruit.

Leave pickles to mature for 3 months before serving. Most will keep for up to 1 year, but red cabbage pickles should be served within 2–3 weeks.

MAKING CHUTNEYS AND RELISHES
These are the simplest preserves to make. All the ingredients, including sugar which gives the sweet-sour flavor, are simmered until there are no pools of liquid left on the surface. For chutneys this can take as long as 4 hours. Only occasional stirring is needed. Jar and process as pickles.

USING THE PRESSURE COOKER

Use the pressure cooker to save time when making preserves. It is especially good for making marmalade and softening hard fruits for jellies. Not only is there a great time saving but the fruit retains its flavor and color beautifully. Always consult manufacturer's instructions before using your pressure cooker for preserving. Although the entire preserve can be made in the pressure cooker pan, only the preliminary cooking and softening of the fruit can be done actually under pressure. After adding the sugar and any lemon juice the preserve must be boiled in the open pan for about 15 minutes. Never fill the pan more than half full; use half the amount of water given in a standard recipe. Add half of this when the fruit is cooked under pressure. The second half is added with the sugar. Cook citrus fruits for 20 minutes at medium (10 lb) pressure. Release pressure at room temperature.

FRUITS IN ALCOHOL

For a delicious dessert that you can boast is homemade, fruits in alcohol are well worth making. They are made by preserving lightly poached fruits like peaches, apricots and plums in equal parts of sugar and alcohol. Brandy is usually used, but try more unusual mixtures containing kirsch or orange-flavored liqueurs. The sugar syrup can be flavored with whole spices like cinnamon and cloves, and for an attractive appearance the spices can be added to the jar. Fruits in alcohol should be filled and covered in the same way as jams.

BUSY COOK'S GUIDE TO JAMS, JELLIES AND MARMALADE

- Cook frozen fruit from frozen to prevent discoloration.

- Chop citrus fruit peel in the chopper attachment of a food mixer or in a food processor. Do not use a coarse grinder as it produces a paste-like marmalade.

- Soak citrus peel overnight to help soften it.

- For jams made with pitted fruits, the pits will float to the surface after cooking and can be removed with a slotted spoon. Cherries are an exception, however, and their pits should be removed beforehand, with a cherry pitter.

- Grease the bottom of the preserving pan with butter to help prevent sticking during cooking.

- Warm the sugar in a 275°F oven before adding it to the fruit and it will dissolve more quickly when stirred into the fruit.

- Have saucers chilling in the refrigerator ready for testing.

- Adding a pat of butter after the sugar has dissolved helps reduce foaming.

- Scald a jelly bag so the fruit juice runs clean through and is not absorbed by the fabric.

- Don't rush the straining by squeezing the bag—this results in a cloudy mixture.

- Wipe filled jars clean while they are still warm with a cloth that has been wrung out in hot water.

PECTIN CONTENT OF FRUITS AND VEGETABLES USED IN PRESERVING

Good	Medium	Poor
Cooking apples	Dessert apples	Bananas
Crabapples	Apricots	Carrots
Cranberries	Blueberries	Cherries
Fresh currants	Blackberries	Elderberries
Gooseberries	Greengage plums	Figs
Lemons	Loganberries	Grapes
Limes	Mulberries	Squash
Oranges	Raspberries	Melons
Plums (some varieties)		Nectarines
Quinces		Peaches
		Pineapple
		Rhubarb
		Strawberries

PRESERVE RECIPES

GOOSEBERRY JELLY

Makes about 4 lb

$4\frac{1}{2}$ lb gooseberries, washed

water

sugar

1 Put the gooseberries in a preserving pan with water to cover. Bring to the boil, then simmer gently for $\frac{3}{4}$–1 hour until the fruit is soft and pulpy. Stir from time to time.

2 Spoon the fruit pulp into a jelly bag or cloth attached to the legs of an upturned stool and leave to strain into a large bowl for at least 12 hours.

3 Discard the pulp remaining in the jelly bag. Measure the extract and return it to the pan with 1 lb sugar for each $2\frac{1}{2}$ cups extract. Heat gently, stirring, until the sugar has dissolved, then boil rapidly for about 15 minutes.

4 Test for a set, then remove any scum with a slotted spoon. Cover and seal.

——————— VARIATIONS ———————

GOOSEBERRY MINT JELLY
Cook the gooseberries with a few sprigs of mint and add finely chopped mint to the jelly before sealing.

GOOSEBERRY AND ELDERFLOWER JELLY
Tie two large elderflower heads in a piece of muslin. When the jelly has reached setting point, remove from the heat, add the muslin bag and stir around in the hot jelly for about 3 minutes. This will produce a good flavor that is not over-dominant.

STRAWBERRY JAM

Makes about 5 lb

$3\frac{1}{2}$ lb strawberries, washed and hulled

3 Tbsp lemon juice

3 lb sugar

pat of butter

1 Put the strawberries in a preserving pan with the lemon juice. Simmer gently, stirring occasionally, for 20–30 minutes until really soft.

2 Take the pan off the heat, add the sugar and stir until dissolved. Add butter and boil rapidly for about 20 minutes.

3 Test for a set, then remove any scum with a slotted spoon.

4 Allow the jam to cool for 15–20 minutes, stir gently, fill jars and cover; process.

APRICOT CONSERVE

Makes about 5 lb

1 lb dried apricots, soaked in 8 cups water overnight

juice of 1 lemon

3 lb sugar

$\frac{1}{2}$ cup blanched almonds, split

pat of butter

1 Put the apricots in a preserving pan with the soaking water and lemon juice. Simmer for about 30 minutes until soft, stirring from time to time.

2 Remove the pan from the heat and add the sugar and almonds. Stir until the sugar has dissolved, then add butter and boil rapidly for 20–25 minutes, stirring frequently to prevent sticking.

3 Test for a set, then remove any scum with a slotted spoon. Fill jars, cover, and process.

ORANGE MARMALADE

Makes about 10 lb

3 lb oranges, washed

juice of 2 lemons

4 quarts water

6 lb sugar

1 Halve the oranges and squeeze out the juice and seeds. Tie the seeds, and any membrane that has come away during squeezing, in a piece of muslin.

2 Slice the orange peel thinly or thickly, as preferred, and put it in a preserving pan with the fruit juices, water and muslin bag. Simmer gently for about 2 hours until the peel is really soft and the liquid reduced by about half.

3 Remove the muslin bag, squeezing it well and allowing the juice to run back into the pan. Add the sugar, stirring until it has dissolved, then boil the mixture rapidly for about 15–20 minutes. Test for a set, then remove any scum with a slotted spoon.

4 Allow the marmalade to cool for 15–20 minutes, stir gently, then fill jars and process.

LEMON CURD

Makes about 1½ lb

finely grated rind and juice of 4
  medium lemons

4 eggs

½ cup butter

2 cups sugar

1 Place all the ingredients in the
  top of a double saucepan or in
a bowl standing over a pan of
simmering water. Stir until the
sugar has dissolved and continue
heating gently for about 20
minutes until the curd thickens.

2 Strain into jars and cover.
  Process. Store for about
1 month only.

———— VARIATION ————

The fresh lemon juice can be
replaced with ¾ cup reconstituted
lemon juice. To give extra tang,
add the grated rind of 1 fresh
lemon.

CORN RELISH

Makes about 5½ lb

6 ears corn

½ a small green cabbage, trimmed
  and roughly chopped

2 medium onions, halved

1½ sweet red peppers, seeded and
  quartered

2 tsp salt

2 Tbsp flour

½ tsp turmeric

1 cup sugar

2 tsp powdered mustard

2½ cups distilled white vinegar

1 Cook the corn in boiling water
  for 3 minutes, then drain.
Using a sharp knife, cut the
kernels from the cobs.

2 Coarsely mince the cabbage,
  onions and red peppers and
combine with the corn.

3 Blend the salt, flour, turmeric,
  sugar and mustard together in
a saucepan, then gradually stir in
the vinegar. Heat gently, stirring,
until the sugar has dissolved, then
bring to the boil. Add the
vegetables and simmer for 25–30
minutes, stirring occasionally.
Cover and refrigerate.

BEET AND HORSERADISH RELISH

Makes about 3 lb

2 oz fresh horseradish

1 lb beets

1 medium onion

8 oz cooking apples

2 cups cider vinegar

1½ cups sugar

1 Peel and grate the horseradish.
  Peel the beets, then shred or
grate coarsely. Chop the onion.
Peel, quarter, core and roughly
chop the apples.

2 Place all the ingredients in a
  medium-sized saucepan and
heat gently until the sugar
dissolves.

3 Boil gently, uncovered, for
  about 1¼ hours until the
ingredients are tender and the
contents well reduced. Cover and
refrigerate.

PICKLED RED CABBAGE

about 3 lb firm red cabbage, finely shredded

2 large onions, sliced

4 Tbsp salt

2½ quarts spiced vinegar (see below)

1 Tbsp light brown sugar

1 Layer the cabbage and onion in a large bowl, sprinkling each layer with salt, then cover and leave overnight.

2 Next day drain the cabbage and onion thoroughly, rinse off the surplus salt and drain again. Pack into jars.

3 Pour the vinegar into a pan and heat gently. Add the sugar and stir until dissolved. Leave to cool, then pour over the cabbage and onion and cover immediately. Use within 2–3 weeks as the cabbage tends to lose its crispness.

SPICED VINEGAR

Makes 5 cups

5 cups vinegar

2 Tbsp mace

1 Tbsp whole allspice

1 Tbsp whole cloves

7 inches cinnamon stick

6 peppercorns

1 small bay leaf

1 Place the vinegar, spices and bay leaf in a saucepan, bring to the boil and pour into a bowl or bottles. Cover to preserve the flavor and leave to marinate for 2 hours.

2 Strain through muslin, pour into clean bottles and seal with airtight and vinegar-proof tops. An even better result is obtained if the spices are left to stand in unheated vinegar for 1–2 months.

DRIED FRUIT PICKLE

Makes about 3 lb

1 lb sugar

1¼ cups distilled white vinegar

2 tsp whole cloves

2 tsp whole allspice

1 cinnamon stick

pared rind of 1 small lemon

½ tsp ground ginger

2 lb dried mixed fruit, soaked in cold water overnight

1 Put the sugar and vinegar in a preserving pan and heat gently until the sugar dissolves.

2 Place the cloves, allspice, cinnamon stick and lemon rind in a muslin bag. Crush lightly.

3 Add the bag to the vinegar and sugar. Stir in the ground ginger and bring to the boil. Cook for 5–7 minutes until reduced and syrupy, with about 3 cups remaining.

4 Put the dried fruit in a separate pan with the soaking water. Cover and simmer until tender. Drain, then pack into warm jars. Cover completely with the hot reduced vinegar. Process.

5 Keep for several weeks before eating. Store in the refrigerator after opening.

PICKLED ONIONS

Makes about 4 lb

4 lb pickling onions

1 lb salt

5 quarts water

5 cups spiced vinegar (see below left)

1 Place the onions, without peeling, in a large bowl. Dissolve half the salt in half the water, pour the brine over the onions and leave for 12 hours.

2 Peel the onions, then cover with fresh brine, made with the remaining salt and water. Leave for a further 24–36 hours.

3 Drain and rinse the onions well and pack them into jars. Pour the spiced vinegar over the onions and cover the jars immediately with airtight and vinegar-proof tops. Process.

TOMATO AND SWEET RED PEPPER CHUTNEY

Makes about 3 lb

2 lb ripe tomatoes

4 medium onions

1 red chili

1 sweet red pepper

1¼ cups distilled white vinegar

⅔ cup raw sugar

1 tsp salt

1 tsp paprika

¼ tsp chili powder

1 Peel and roughly chop the tomatoes and onions. Seed and finely chop the chili and pepper.

2 Place all the ingredients in a medium saucepan and heat gently until the sugar dissolves.

3 Boil gently, uncovered, for about 1½ hours until the vegetables are tender and the chutney of a thick pulpy consistency, stirring occasionally. Cover and refrigerate.

COOK-AHEAD AND THE FREEZER

A freezer is a great aid to cooking ahead if kept well stocked with pre-cooked dishes, meat packs, vegetables and other ingredients including pastry and bread doughs.

Good freezer candidates are stews, casseroles, soups, stocks, sauces, cooked meats, fruit pies, bread and cakes: anything that takes too long to prepare when dinnertime is only 30 minutes away, freezes well and can then be served up quickly after thawing. But be careful to choose things your family will always eat: a good practice is to cook double or triple amounts of favorite dishes, serve one and freeze the rest.

A few points to remember when cooking for the freezer: with stews, add watery vegetables like zucchini when reheating; also potatoes, rice and pasta in case of overcooking. Frozen fat can spoil flavor, so degrease after chilling.

Add light cream, sour cream and yogurt on reheating, as they separate during freezing, create extra volume and waste space. Freeze soups as purées and add stock, milk or cream to thin down before serving. Season dishes on reheating as freezing affects the flavor of spices and seasonings.

When cooking in bulk be sure you have done all necessary shopping and that there is space for open freezing and storing what you make. Don't overload the freezer as food must freeze quickly to prevent large ice crystals forming. They damage food and alter flavor, texture and even color. Too much food at a time slows freezing down. Follow the maker's instructions on using the fast freeze switch. As a general rule freeze no more than a tenth of your freezer's capacity. This means that you should freeze no more than 10 lb of food in a 110 lb (6 cubic feet) freezer.

PACKING

Pack food in practical serving portions. You may want a few larger dinner-party packs, and if your family has an irregular time schedule, then a few single portions may be in order—especially useful if you heat food in a microwave. Remember that several packs can be reheated, but one large portion may only produce unwanted leftovers. Smaller portions also thaw and heat more quickly than large ones. Use shallow containers for food for the same reason—the deeper the container filled with food the longer it will take to thaw and heat.

Interleaving pancakes with paper

Single items of food like fish fillets or pancakes should be packed with paper interleaved between them and then wrapped so that you can remove only those required at one time. Consider also whether it suits your family to freeze cakes and cooked fruit pies in serving portions rather than

Packing cake in serving portions

whole, and pack them accordingly.

Using liners is an excellent way to freeze liquid dishes. They are especially good for freezing soups and casseroles, freeing the container for another use, and they also take up a minimum of freezer space. Line a casserole or other

Lining casserole dish with foil

rigid container with foil and pour or spoon in the food to be frozen. Once frozen, the contents can be removed, overwrapped, and returned to the freezer. When it is time to serve the dish it can be neatly inserted into the original dish and reheated.

When freezing stews, casseroles or fruits in syrup, solid pieces should be completely submerged in the liquid with no protruding pieces otherwise they may get freezer burn. As with all liquid dishes, always leave $\frac{1}{2}$ inch headspace to allow for expansion during freezing. With other foods all air must be excluded from the packages. Heat sealing in a secure way to seal plastic bags and they make convenient boil-in-the-bags.

Along with the date and contents, labels should give information about finishing the dish such as adding seasonings, thickening or any liquid.

THAWING AND REHEATING

Most cooked dishes can be reheated from frozen and this helps to preserve flavor, texture and color. Cooking from frozen is essential for vegetables, but other cooked dishes can be thawed before reheating. This is more of an economy measure than anything else, for example, to reheat a stew from frozen needs 1 hour in a 400°F oven, then a further 40 minutes at 350°F. A thawed stew will only need 20–40 minutes at 350°F. Reheating can also be done on the stove. If frozen, break up chunks with a fork to speed up reheating. Do not re-freeze thawed raw food unless it is cooked first, cooled quickly, then frozen.

FREEZER STANDBYS

Have these on hand to save time on last-minute preparations. This is a great way to use up leftovers.

STOCKS AND SAUCES

Make your own bouillon cubes by

Storing frozen bouillon cubes

freezing stock in ice-cube trays until solid, then storing them in plastic bags (a well-reduced stock will be concentrated in flavor). Use as a convenient way to flavor soups and stews. Cubes of left-over sauces are also handy for flavoring.

CHEESE

Pack grated cheese in a plastic bag; the cheese will stay separate so you can shake out only as much as needed.

CHOCOLATE

When you feel like indulging in a little chocolate cookery, make chocolate squares, curls or leaves; freeze in rigid containers, inter-leaving layers to prevent crushing.

Interleaving chocolate shapes

Use for decoration while still very cold, but allow 10 minutes to thaw.

WHIPPED CREAM

Freeze leftover cream by piping in rosettes onto baking parchment

Piping rosettes onto baking parchment

on a tray. Open freeze until solid, then pack in rigid containers, interleaving layers to prevent crushing. Use from frozen to decorate, but allow 10 minutes to thaw.

JUICE OR RIND OF ORANGES AND LEMONS

When using just the rind or the juice of citrus fruits in a recipe, freeze the unused parts in a small container. For convenience in later recipes, make sure you state the quantity for each portion frozen. Grate rind before freezing.

BREADCRUMBS

Make fresh breadcrumbs and pack in plastic bags—the crumbs will stay separate. Thaw for 30 minutes if using to coat for frying, otherwise use from frozen. Buttered crumbs can also be frozen ready for use as toppings to

be browned under the grill. Open freeze, then pack in plastic bags in useable quantities.

CROÛTONS

Open freeze on trays until solid, then pack in a plastic bag. Reheat from frozen for 5–10 minutes in the oven at 400°F.

HERBS

Freeze whole sprigs of herbs, then, to avoid chopping them, crumble while still frozen into soups and stews; herbs will be too wet to use as a garnish.

Crumbling frozen herbs into soup

Alternatively, freeze chopped herbs with water in ice-cube trays (as for stock above), then transfer to a plastic bag.

Use straight from the freezer as an addition to stews, casseroles and sauces.

BUTTER BALLS

These take time to make when needed, but a few stored in the freezer—even those left over from a party—are handy for almost instant use.

PARSLEY BUTTER

This is ideal for topping steaks, chops and other grills such as fish. Cream $\frac{1}{2}$ cup unsalted butter until smooth. Beat in the grated rind and juice of 1 lemon, 4 Tbsp chopped fresh parsley, and salt and pepper. Form into a long sausage shape between sheets of waxed or non-stick paper. Refirm in the fridge or freezer and cut into 4-Tbsp portions. Wrap each in foil. Alternatively, freeze the butter roll whole and cut off slices as required. Make a neat parcel, seal and label. Use straight from the freezer.

Basic Recipes

These recipes for stocks, sauces and dressings can all be made in advance. The pancakes, pastries and crumble topping can even be frozen for later use.

STOCKS, SAUCES AND DRESSINGS

CHICKEN STOCK

Makes 5–6 cups

carcass and bones of a cooked chicken

6–7 cups cold water

1 onion, sliced

1 carrot, peeled and sliced

1 celery stalk, washed, trimmed and sliced

bouquet garni (optional)

1 Break down the carcass and bones of the cooked chicken, and make sure to include any skin and chicken scraps.

2 Put in a pan with the water, onion, carrot, celery and the bouquet garni, if using.

3 Bring to the boil, skim with a slotted spoon, then cover and simmer for 3 hours.

4 Strain the stock thoroughly, discarding the bones and vegetables, then leave to cool. When cold, remove all traces of fat.

BEEF STOCK

Makes about 6 cups

1 lb shin of beef, cut into pieces

1 lb marrow bone or knuckle of veal, chopped

7 cups cold water

bouquet garni

1 onion, sliced

1 carrot, peeled and sliced

1 celery stalk, washed, trimmed and sliced

1 To give a good flavor and color, brown the bones and meat in the oven (exact temperature is not important) before using.

2 Put in a pan with the water, bouquet garni and vegetables. Bring to the boil, skim with a slotted spoon, then cover and simmer for 5–6 hours.

3 Strain the stock thoroughly, discarding the bones, meat and vegetables, then leave to cool. When cold, remove all traces of fat.

BASIC WHITE SAUCE

Makes 1¼ cups

1 Tbsp butter

2 Tbsp flour

1¼ cups milk

salt and freshly ground pepper

1 Melt the butter in a saucepan. Add the flour and cook over low heat, stirring with a wooden spoon, for 2 minutes. Do not allow the mixture (roux) to brown.

2 Remove the pan from the heat and gradually blend in the milk, stirring after each addition to prevent lumps forming. Bring to the boil slowly and continue to cook, stirring all the time, until the sauce comes to the boil and thickens.

3 Once thickened, simmer the sauce very gently for a further 2–3 minutes. Season with salt and freshly ground pepper.

COATING SAUCE

Follow recipe for Basic White Sauce (see left), but increase butter and flour by 1 Tbsp each.

CHEESE SAUCE

Follow the recipe for the Basic White Sauce or Coating Sauce (see above). Before seasoning, stir in ½ cup grated Cheddar cheese and ½ tsp mustard.

MAYONNAISE

Makes about 1½ cups

3 egg yolks
1½ tsp dry mustard
1½ tsp salt
½ tsp freshly ground pepper
1½ tsp sugar (optional)
2 cups sunflower oil or ½ olive oil and ½ vegetable oil
3 Tbsp white wine vinegar or lemon juice

1 Put the egg yolks in a bowl with the seasonings and sugar and beat with a whisk. Continue beating and add ⅔ cup of the oil about a drop at a time.

2 Once the mixture starts to thicken, continue adding the oil in a thin stream. Add the vinegar or lemon juice, beating constantly.

3 Add the remaining oil 1 Tbsp at a time or in a thin stream, beating continually until it is completely absorbed.

TOMATO MAYONNAISE

Prepare as above, but add **2 tomatoes**, peeled, seeded and diced; **3 small spring onions**, trimmed and chopped; ¾ tsp salt and 1 Tbsp vinegar.

GARLIC MAYONNAISE

Peel **2 medium-sized garlic cloves** and crush with some of the salt; add to the mayonnaise.

CUCUMBER MAYONNAISE

Prepared as above but add **6 Tbsp** finely chopped cucumber and 1½ tsp salt.

FRENCH DRESSING

Makes about 1¼ cups

5 Tbsp red or white wine vinegar*
2 tsp Dijon or prepared English mustard
2 tsp salt
1 tsp freshly ground pepper
2 tsp sugar (optional)
2 garlic cloves, crushed (optional)
1 cup oil*

1 For a creamy dressing blend the ingredients in an electric blender or food processor.

2 For a thinner dressing, shake vigorously in a screw-topped jar.

* Try also **tarragon vinegar** in dressings for tomatoes or potatoes; **thyme vinegar** with eggs or mushrooms; **cider vinegar** with fruits. **Lemon juice** can be substituted for vinegar as well.

* **Sunflower oil** alone or half and half with **olive oil** is pleasant. **Walnut oil** also adds interest.

PANCAKES, PASTRIES AND TOPPINGS

CRUMBLE TOPPING

Serves 4–6

1¼ cups flour
6 Tbsp margarine or butter
⅓ cup sugar

Put the flour in a bowl, then rub in the fat with the fingertips until the mixture is the texture of fine crumbs. Stir in the sugar.

This mixture may be kept in the refrigerator for 3–4 days; it can also be frozen—pack in a plastic bag and freeze for up to 3 months.

Add **1 tsp ground cinnamon, mixed spices** or **ginger** to the flour before rubbing in the fat.

Add ½ **cup chopped crystallized ginger** to the crumb mixture before using.

Add the **finely grated rind of 1 orange or lemon** to the crumb mixture before using.

Roughly crush **2 Tbsp cornflakes** and add them to the rubbed-in mixture with **light brown sugar** in place of granulated sugar.

PANCAKES

Makes 8 pancakes

¾ cup flour

pinch of salt

1 egg

1¼ cups milk

shortening or vegetable oil

1 Mix the flour and salt together in a bowl. Make a well in the center and break in the egg. Add half the liquid, then gradually work in the flour from the sides of the bowl. Beat until smooth.

2 Add the remaining liquid gradually. Beat until the ingredients are well mixed.

3 Heat a little shortening or oil in a small frying pan, running it around the pan to coat the sides. Pour in a little batter, tilting the pan to form an even coating.

4 Place over moderate heat and cook until golden underneath, then turn with a palette knife and cook the other side. Slide the pancake on to a plate lined with waxed paper. Repeat.

PIECRUST PASTRY

1¼ cups flour

pinch of salt

6 Tbsp butter or margarine

about 2 Tbsp cold water

1 Mix the flour and salt together in a bowl. Cut the fat into small pieces and add it to the flour.

2 Using both hands, rub the fat into the flour between finger and thumb tips until the mixture resembles fine breadcrumbs.

3 Add the water, sprinkling it evenly over the surface. Stir it in with a round-bladed knife until the mixture begins to stick together in large lumps.

4 With one hand, collect the mixture together and knead lightly for a few seconds to give a firm, smooth dough. The pastry can be used straight away, but is better allowed to "rest" for about 30 minutes. It can also be wrapped in plastic and kept in the refrigerator for a day or two.

5 *To roll out:* sprinkle a very little flour on a working surface and the rolling pin, not on the pastry, and roll out the dough evenly in one direction only, turning it occasionally. The ideal thickness is usually about ⅛ inch. Do not pull or stretch the pastry. When cooking shortcrust pastry, the usual oven temperature is 400–425°F.

SWEET PIE CRUST PASTRY

¾ cup flour

pinch of salt

6 Tbsp butter or margarine

1 tsp sugar

1 egg, beaten

1 Mix the flour and salt together in a bowl. Cut the fat into small pieces, add it to the flour and rub it in as for shortcrust pastry until the mixture resembles fine breadcrumbs. Stir in the sugar until evenly mixed.

2 Add the egg, stirring with a round-bladed knife until the ingredients begin to stick together in large lumps.

3 With one hand, collect the mixture together and knead lightly for a few seconds to give a firm, smooth dough.

4 Rest and roll out as for shortcrust pastry and use as required. When cooking pie pastry the usual oven temperature is 400°F.

ROUGH PUFF PASTRY

1½ cups flour

pinch of salt

6 Tbsp butter or margarine

6 Tbsp lard

about ⅔ cup cold water

squeeze of lemon juice

beaten egg, to glaze

1 Mix the flour and salt together in a bowl. Cut the fat (which should be quite firm) into cubes about ¾ inch across.

2 Stir the fat into the flour without breaking up the pieces. Add enough water and lemon juice to mix to a fairly stiff dough.

3 Turn the dough on to a lightly floured surface, then roll out into an oblong three times as long as it is wide. Fold the bottom third up and the top third down.

4 Turn the pastry so that the folded edges are at the sides. Seal the ends of the pastry by pressing lightly with a rolling pin.

5 Repeat this rolling and folding process three more times, turning the dough so that the folded edge is on the left hand side each time.

6 Wrap the pastry loosely in waxed paper and leave it to rest in the refrigerator or a cool place for about 30 minutes before using.

7 Roll out the pastry on a lightly floured surface to ⅛ inch thick and use as required. Brush with beaten egg before baking. The usual oven temperature for rough puff pastry is 425°F.

PUFF PASTRY

4 cups bread flour
pinch of salt
1 lb butter
about 1¼ cups cold water
1 Tbsp lemon juice
beaten egg, to glaze

1 Mix the bread flour and pinch of salt together in a large bowl.

2 Cut 4 Tbsp off the butter and pat the remainder with a rolling pin into a slab ¾ inch thick.

3 Rub the 4 Tbsp butter into the flour with the finger and thumb tips. Stir in enough water and lemon juice to make a soft, elastic dough.

4 Turn the dough on to a lightly floured surface, then knead until smooth. Shape into a round and cut through half the depth in a cross shape.

5 Open out the flaps to form a star. Roll out, keeping the center four times as thick as the flaps.

6 Place the slab of butter in the center of the dough and fold over the flaps, envelope-style. Press gently with the rolling pin.

7 Roll out into a rectangle measuring about 16 × 8 inches. Fold the bottom third up and the top third down, keeping the edges straight. Seal the edges by pressing with the rolling pin.

8 Wrap the pastry loosely in waxed paper and leave it to rest in the refrigerator or a cool place for about 30 minutes.

9 Put the pastry on a lightly floured surface with the folded edges to the sides and repeat the rolling, folding and resting sequence five times.

10 After the final resting, roll out the pastry on a lightly floured surface and shape as required. Brush with beaten egg before baking. The usual oven temperature for puff pastry is 450°F.

FLAKY PASTRY

1½ cups flour
pinch of salt
6 Tbsp butter or margarine
6 Tbsp lard
about ⅔ cup cold water
squeeze of lemon juice
beaten egg, to glaze

1 Mix the flour and salt together in a bowl. Soften the fat by working it with a knife on a plate, then divide it into four equal portions.

2 Add one quarter of the fat to the flour and rub it in between finger and thumb tips until the mixture resembles fine breadcrumbs.

3 Add enough water and lemon juice to make a soft elastic dough, stirring it in with a round-bladed knife.

4 Turn the dough on to a lightly floured surface and roll out into an oblong three times as long as it is wide.

5 Using the round-bladed knife, dot another quarter of the fat over the top two-thirds of the pastry in flakes, so that it looks like buttons on a card.

6 Fold the bottom third of the pastry up and the top third down, and turn it so that the folded edges are at the side. Seal the edges of the pastry by pressing with a rolling pin.

7 Re-roll as before and repeat the process twice more until the remaining portions of fat have been used up.

8 Wrap the pastry loosely in waxed paper and leave it to rest in the refrigerator or a cool place for at least 30 minutes before using.

9 Roll out the pastry on a lightly floured surface to ⅛ inch thick and use as required. Brush with beaten egg before baking. The usual oven temperature for flaky pastry is 425°F.

PÂTE SUCRÉE

¾ cup flour
pinch of salt
⅓ cup sugar
4 Tbsp butter, at room temperature
2 egg yolks

1 Sift the flour and salt together onto a cool surface, ideally a marble slab.

2 Make a well in the center of the mixture and add the sugar, butter and egg yolks.

3 Using the fingertips of one hand, pinch and work the sugar, butter and egg yolks together until well blended. Gradually work in all the flour, adding a little water if necessary to bind it together.

4 Turn the dough on to a lightly floured surface and knead lightly until smooth. Wrap loosely in foil or plastic and leave it to rest in the refrigerator or a cool place for about 1 hour.

5 Roll out the pastry on a lightly floured surface and use as required. The usual oven temperature for pâte sucrée is 375°F.

BAKING BLIND

Baking blind is the process of baking a pastry case without the filling—essential if the filling is to be uncooked or if it only requires a short cooking time. First shape the pastry into the baking tin. Prick the pastry base with a fork. For large cases, cut a piece of aluminum foil rather larger than the tin. Use this to line the pastry and weight it down with some dried beans, pasta or rice.

Alternatively, crumple a piece of foil and use that to line the base of the pastry case. Bake the pastry at the temperature given in the recipe for 10–15 minutes, then remove the baking beans and paper, or the foil lining, and return the tin to the oven for a further 5 minutes to crisp the pastry. Leave the baked case to cool and shrink slightly before removing it from the tin. (The baking beans can be kept for use again.)

For small cases, it is usually sufficient to prick the pastry well with a fork before baking.

Baked unfilled pastry cases can be kept for a few days in an airtight container.

INDEX